The Birdwatcher's Activity Book

THE
BIRDWATCHER'S
ACTIVITY BOOK

Donald S. Heintzelman

Stackpole Books

Published by
STACKPOLE BOOKS
Cameron and Kelker Streets
P. O. Box 1831
Harrisburg, PA 17105

Printed in the U.S.A.

Library of Congress Cataloging in Publication Data

Heintzelman, Donald S.
    The birdwatcher's activity book.

    Includes bibliographies and index.
    1. Bird watching. I. Title.
QL677.5.H43   1982   598'.07'234   82-19201
ISBN 0-8117-2152-3 (pbk.)

Contents

Preface

There was a time, not too many years ago, when looking at birds was considered odd by a large segment of the American public. Not any more! Today thanks to the field guides written by Roger Tory Peterson and others, we live in the Age of Bird Watching as I pointed out not long ago in *A Manual for Bird Watching in the Americas*—itself a book that presents a wide spectrum of bird-watching facts, figures, and suggestions on this most exciting of natural history hobbies.

This book, however, explores a sampling of bird-watching projects and activities not included in my earlier Manual. *The Birdwatcher's Activity Book,* therefore, suggests avenues on which one may enjoy added dimension to the already rich hobby of bird watching. It is designed to encourage people to enjoy unusual or new bird-watching projects and activities—to set people thinking about ways in which they can advance the cause of bird watching, study, conservation, and related activities in North America and elsewhere.

The selection of projects and activities included in this book is arbitrary. The choice is mine. Perhaps other projects and activities will appear in a companion volume at a later date. For the moment, however, the material contained in this book is adequate to stimulate many birdwatchers to look into many corners of bird watching not normally examined.

During the preparation of this book, I referred to several earlier books of mine including *Autumn Hawk Flights, A Guide to Hawk Watching in North America, Hawks and Owls of North America, A Manual for Bird Watching in the Americas, North American Ducks, Geese & Swans,* and *The Illustrated Bird Watcher's Dictionary.* Additional reference was made to a number of other books and these are mentioned in the text at appropriate places or in the Additional Reading lists at the end of each chapter.

Reference also was made to information published in the following periodicals: *American Birds, Auk, Birding, Bird Watcher's Digest, Bulletin Tall Timbers Research Station, Cassinia, Defenders, Field & Stream, Living Bird, Misc. Publications of the Museum of Zoology, University of Michigan, National Geographic, National Wildlife, New Jersey Nature News, North American Fauna, Prints, Sierra Club Newsletter,* and the *Wilson Bulletin.*

A portion of chapter 3 is adapted from an article of mine entitled "The Birder and Ecological Niche," first published in a 1973 issue of *New Jersey Nature News.*

Of the various photographs used to illustrate this book, those not credited are mine. Photographs taken by others are credited appropriately to the proper agency, institution, or person.

Appreciation also is extended to the Federation of New York State Bird Clubs, Inc., for permission to reprint their waterfowl survey form.

Allentown, Pennsylvania   Donald S. Heintzelman

Chapter 1

Bird-Watching Basics

Watching wild birds as a hobby requires not only the skills needed to identify birds correctly, but also the knowledge needed to know where various bird species live, when to expect to see certain species, and how to go about seeing them. In other words, mastery of bird-watching basics is fundamental to enjoying recreational bird watching to the fullest extent possible.

Advanced birdwatchers already will know the information presented in this chapter, but even they can profit from a review of the basics. Less advanced and beginning birders, however, will profit by studying and learning all of the bird-watching basics discussed here.

FIELD GUIDES

Birdwatchers in North America are extremely fortunate because they have available several excellent general field guides to bird identification. Every birdwatcher should own at least one

Student birdwatchers learning the fundamentals of bird identification by gaining field experience.

of these basic books, and it is helpful to have several, if possible, since no single guide provides all of the helpful information. Fundamental, however, are the following:

A Field Guide to the Birds by Roger Tory Peterson.

A Field Guide to Western Birds by Roger Tory Peterson.

A Guide to Field Identification/Birds of North America by Chandler S. Robbins, Bertel Bruun, Herbert S. Zim, and Arthur Singer.

Less useful, but containing fine color photographs of birds, are the eastern and western editions of *The Audubon Society Field Guide to North American Birds* by John Bull and Miklos D. F. Udvardy respectively.

Because diurnal birds of prey are extremely popular birds and difficult to identify, I also recommend my own *A Guide to Hawk Watching in North America* because it presents many fine points of hawk identification not contained in any of the standard general bird identification guides.

In addition to these basic books, a wide variety of others dealing with various aspects of birds are available. A summary is provided in *A Manual for Bird Watching in the Americas* which serves as companion volume to this book.

IDENTIFICATION

Learning to identify wild birds is fundamental and necessary before other aspects of bird watching, including some of the projects discussed in this book, can be explored. Thus it is worthwhile to review the basics of bird identification first.

Basic Bird Groups

Even the most inexperienced person starting out in bird watching probably knows more about bird identification than is realized. Certainly most people are able to recognize some basic bird groups such as geese or ducks, pigeons, owls, and sparrows although they may not know which species in those groups are being seen. Nevertheless, part of one of the first tasks in becoming a bird-watcher is mastered—recognition of basic bird groups. Of course, it also is necessary to learn all of the basic groups likely to occur in an area—perhaps one's county or state—in order to advance as a birder. This task is neither overly difficult nor impossible, especially with the aid of one or several excellent general field guides to North American bird identification. Roger Tory Peterson, for example, lists the following eight bird groups in *A Field Guide to the Birds*.

1. *Swimmers*—Ducks, loons, grebes, coots
2. *Aerialists*—Gulls and terns
3. *Long-legged Waders*—Herons, egrets, cranes
4. *Small Waders*—Shorebirds (plovers, sandpipers)
5. *Upland Game Birds*—Grouse, quail, turkeys
6. *Birds of Prey*—Vultures, hawks, eagles, owls
7. *Non-perching Birds*—Swifts, hummingbirds, kingfishers, woodpeckers
8. *Perching Birds*—Flycatchers, thrushes, warblers, sparrows

To a beginner, these eight bird groups may seem adequate. With

The Screech Owl, a bird of prey, is a member of one of the eight basic groups of birds recommended by Roger Tory Peterson as aids to learning bird identification.

a little experience, however, it quickly becomes obvious that recognition of representatives of most of the North American bird families is even more helpful in tracking down the correct identification of a particular bird. These families are listed here.

Loons—Family Gaviidae
Grebes—Family Podicipedidae
Albatrosses—Family Diomedeidae
Shearwaters and Petrels—Family Procellariidae
Storm Petrels—Family Hydrobatidae
Tropicbirds—Family Phaethontidae
Pelicans—Family Pelecanidae
Boobies and Gannets—Family Sulidae
Cormorants—Family Phalacrocoracidae
Darters—Family Anhingidae
Frigatebirds—Family Fregatidae
Herons and Bitterns—Family Ardeidae
Storks—Family Ciconiidae
Ibises and Spoonbills—Family Threskiornithidae
Flamingos—Family Phoenicopteridae
Swans, Geese, and Ducks—Family Anatidae
New World Vultures—Family Cathartidae
Kites, Hawks, Eagles, and Harriers—Family Accipitridae
Osprey—Family Pandionidae
Caracaras and Falcons—Family Falconidae
Chachalacas—Family Cracidae
Grouse and Ptarmigan—Family Tetraonidae
Quail and Pheasants—Family Phasianidae
Turkeys—Family Meleagrididae
Cranes—Family Gruidae
Limpkins—Family Aramidae
Rails, Gallinules, and Coots—Family Rallidae
Jacanas—Family Jacanidae
Oystercatchers—Family Haematopodidae
Stilts and Avocets—Family Recurvirostridae
Thick-knees—Family Burhinidae
Plovers—Family Charadriidae
Sandpipers and Phalaropes—Family Scolopacidae
Jaegers and Skuas—Family Stercorariidae

Gulls and Terns—Family Laridae
Skimmers—Family Rynchopidae
Auks and Puffins—Family Alcidae
Pigeons and Doves—Family Columbidae
Parrots—Family Psittacidae
Cuckoos, Roadrunners, and Anis—Family Cuculidae
Barn Owls—Family Tytonidae
Typical Owls—Family Strigidae
Goatsuckers—Family Caprimulgidae
Swifts—Family Apodidae
Hummingbirds—Family Trochilidae
Trogons—Family Trogonidae
Kingfishers—Family Alcedinidae
Woodpeckers and Wrynecks—Family Picidae
Cotingas—Family Cotingidae
Tyrant Flycatchers—Family Tyrannidae
Larks—Family Alaudidae
Swallows—Family Hirundinidae
Jays, Magpies, and Crows—Family Corvidae
Titmice, Verdins, and Bushtits—Family Paridae
Nuthatches—Family Sittidae
Creepers—Family Certhiidae
Wrentits—Family Chamaeidae
Bulbuls—Family Pycnonotidae
Dippers—Family Cinclidae
Wrens—Family Troglodytidae
Mockingbirds and Thrashers—Family Mimidae
Thrushes—Family Turdidae
Old World Warblers, Gnatcatchers, and Kinglets—Family
   Sylviidae
Old World Flycatchers—Family Muscicapidae
Accentors—Family Prunellidae
Wagtails and Pipits—Family Motacillidae
Waxwings—Family Bombycillidae
Silky Flycatchers—Family Ptilogonatidae
Shrikes—Family Laniidae
Starlings—Family Sturnidae
Vireos—Family Vireonidae
Honeycreepers—Family Coerebidae

Wood Warblers—Family Parulidae
Weaver Finches—Family Ploceidae
Meadowlarks, Blackbirds, and Orioles—Family Icteridae
Tanagers—Family Thraupidae
Grosbeaks, Finches, Sparrows, and Buntings—Family
   Fringillidae

Once a birdwatcher is able to place most of the birds observed in their correct families, which is a skill that develops rapidly with field experience, tracking down the correct specific identification of a bird is usually relatively easy, since field guides are organized in a sequence of bird families (which may differ somewhat in arrangement in different guides).

FIELD MARKS

The next step in identifying a bird is to determine its unique field marks—the physical and/or behavior features that separate it from all other species. To do this, it is essential to look for certain key features discussed here.

Size

How large is the bird? Is it very large, like an eagle or vulture? Or, is it much smaller like a dove, American Robin, or smaller still like a sparrow?

Shape

What is the bird's shape? Which of the eight basic bird groups does it most resemble? Even very rough placement in a group helps to eliminate many incorrect species and thus speeds arrival at the final correct specific identification. Clearly, eagles or other birds of prey have one more or less typical shape which is much different from the shape of a duck or sparrow. If the bird is flying overhead, the shape of its wings also can be helpful. Falcons, for example, have long pointed wings, quail rounded wings, etc.

The shape of a bird can be a clue to its identification. These American White Pelicans, with their distinctive shape, are nesting in Nevada. Photo by U. S. Fish and Wildlife Service.

Bill

Various species of birds have a remarkable variety of shapes and sizes of bills. Shape of a bird's bill, therefore, can be another helpful clue to identification. Some typical shapes include hook-tipped on birds of prey, long and pointed on terns, small and pointed on wood warblers, and short and stout on sparrows. Keep in mind, however, that on very rare occasions abnormal bills develop on birds, but this factor usually is unimportant in making an identification of most birds.

Tail

The shape and size of a bird's tail also is a helpful field mark. Among the variations in shape are tails that are deeply forked as

The shape of a bird's bill can help to arrive at the correct identification of a species. This bird is a Mourning Dove.

in a Magnificent Frigatebird's, Common Tern's, Swallow-tailed Kite's, or Barn Swallow's. Others may be square-tipped as in some Sharp-shinned Hawks. Still others can be notched as in a Tree Swallow's. Some species have rounded tails as do typical Cooper's Hawks or Blue Jays. Long, pointed tails are another possibility as on the Mourning Dove or Black-billed Magpie. Wedge-shaped tails also occur on some birds as, for example, Northern Gannets. Look at tail shape carefully, therefore, for clues to a bird's identification.

Coloration

A bird's color, or patterns of coloration, also is extremely important in helping a birdwatcher identify a species correctly. Some birds, such as male Northern Cardinals or male Scarlet Tanagers, have very distinctive colors that instantly enable a birdwatcher to recognize them. Other species are so drab or similar in color-

ation that only voice will enable a birdwatcher to identify them—
an example being some of the *Empidonax* flycatchers, especially
Willow and Alder Flycatchers. In most cases, however, unique
combinations of colors allow birdwatchers to recognize the various species they see and it is these field marks that are illustrated
in field guides. They are the patterns of coloration that one must
learn to recognize as being distinctive to a particular species.

In addition to general patterns of coloration, sometimes certain
species also have marks that are of particular field identification
importance—field marks. The white tip of the tail of the Eastern
Kingbird or the yellow tip on the Cedar Waxwing are excellent
field marks for these species. Other species, like towhees or jun-
cos, have white outer tail feathers that attract one's attention.
Some birds, like flickers, have white rump patches. Many birds
have eye-stripes and eye-rings and particular attention must be
given to these field marks if a bird has them. The Northern Goshawk, for example, has a conspicuous white eye-stripe and the
Connecticut Warbler has a white eye-ring. Striped crowns also
are field marks for some species such as the Lark Sparrow and
White-throated Sparrow, among many others. Wing bars also are
important field marks in some species including some vireos and
many wood warblers. Learn to look for these marks, then combine
their presence or absence with the bird's other field marks in
order to identify the species. Sometimes wing patterns also are
important field marks, especially among many shorebirds and
some waterfowl.

Behavior

In some instances a bird's behavior, its physical actions, is
important as a field mark. Wrens cock their tails. Hawks in the
genus *Accipiter* fly with alternating patterns of flapping, sailing,
then more flapping. Creepers climb trees in spiral patterns. Nuthatches hang upside down on trees. American Kestrels, Belted
Kingfishers, and some other species sometimes hover while hunting. Loons, diving ducks, and some other species dive under-
water. But Mallards and many other ducks swim on the surface
and merely dabble for food. Herons and egrets wade into the
water with their long legs designed for this purpose. Some birds,
e.g., American Goldfinches and woodpeckers, fly with undulating

Wing patterns, as on many species of waterfowl including these Mallards, are helpful field marks.

patterns. Bird behavior, therefore, can be an important field mark in some species and it is the task of birdwatchers to learn to know which species exhibit such distinctive field mark behavior.

Song, of course, also is behavior. Each species has its own species-typical song patterns—some much more distinctive than others. Learn to recognize as many bird songs as possible, perhaps by listening to recordings of bird songs. Many experienced birdwatchers do much of their birding by listening to birds sing. In addition to serving as important aids to identification, the songs of birds also are delightful to hear and much of the pleasure of recreational bird watching will be lost if a person does not learn at least the most common songs of the birds of one's home area. Some species, particularly thrushes, are especially beautiful. I never tire of listening to the voice of the Wood Thrush, and the sound of a Northern Cardinal on a late winter day adds meaning to life.

BIRD FINDING

In addition to learning to recognize the field marks of birds, it also is helpful to know where the various species are likely to be found. Learn to know the habitats in which birds normally live. Field guides provide summaries of their habitat requirements, and field experience will soon instill in birders knowledge of where birds normally live.

There also are various books that are aids to bird finding. The most important of these are those written by Olin Sewall Pettingill, Jr. under the titles of *A Guide to Bird Finding East of the Mississippi* and *A Guide to Bird Finding West of the Mississippi*. Every bird watcher should own at least one of these books. For a detailed listing of outstanding hawk migration lookouts, consult *A Guide to Hawk Watching in North America*. A variety of other regional and state bird finding guides also are available and are listed in *A Manual for Bird Watching in the Americas*. New bird-finding guides also are appearing from time to time with notices of their publication appearing in many bird-watching magazines. Many of these also are worthwhile and helpful in leading bird-watchers to locations that are particularly productive birding sites.

ADDITIONAL BASICS

A variety of additional basic bird-watching considerations also are worthwhile to keep in mind. For instance, it is important to know when to visit some locations to enjoy the best birding opportunities that a particular site can offer. In general, the spring (April to early June) and/or autumn (September to late November) migration seasons tend to produce the largest number of species at most locations. Most eastern North American hawk migration lookouts, for example, are noted for their impressive autumn hawk flights. That is the time when most birdwatchers plan to visit places like Bake Oven Knob and Hawk Mountain in eastern Pennsylvania, Cape May Point in southern New Jersey, and the Hawk Ridge Nature Reserve in Minnesota. However, a few hawk lookouts, including Braddock Bay and Derby Hill in New York, are noted for their spring hawk flights rather than large autumn raptor migrations. Much the same also applies to other species of birds. Knowing when to visit refuges or other local birding locations will greatly add to one's birding rewards. Of course not all of the best bird-watching opportunities occur in spring or autumn. One would plan a visit to Bonaventure Island, Quebec in mid-summer to see the thousands of nesting Northern Gannets at that famous seabird refuge. On the other hand, many of our national wildlife refuges produce very large concentrations of waterfowl in late autumn and winter.

Beginning and intermediate level birdwatchers also should consider joining a local group of birders so that they can gain experience and aid from people who usually know more about bird watching, and bird identification and finding, than they do. But after a reasonable amount of birding skill is developed, many birdwatchers prefer to venture afield alone to enjoy the maximum amount of pleasure from bird watching. Nevertheless, some birders always prefer to join groups, so whether to bird watch alone or with others is a matter of personal wishes.

As to necessary equipment, the basics are minimal. One needs a field guide, already discussed, and a satisfactory pair of binoculars. Generally 7×35, 7×50, or 8×40 center-focus binoculars are used by most birdwatchers. In my own activities, however, I use 10×40 binoculars for all my bird-watching activities. Plan on paying no less than about $100.00 for a pair of binoculars. Those costing considerably less may not be well constructed. On the other hand, the very finest binoculars are superb optical instruments but they cost as much as $1,000.00 depending upon the type one buys. Beginning and intermediate level birdwatchers do not need such expensive instruments, but as one's interest in bird watching grows, some consideration might be given to the purchase of a very fine pair of binoculars.

Many birdwatchers also use telescopes, especially with 20X magnification, to aid them in identification of birds seen at a distance such as shorebirds on mudflats far away or hawks at a distance. Generally telescopes are mounted on firm photographic tripods. Bushnell and Swift brands seem to be the most widely used types of telescopes seen and purchased in photographic shops. A further discussion of basic bird-watching equipment is provided in *A Manual for Bird Watching in the Americas.*

ADDITIONAL READING

Bull, J. and J. Farrand, Jr.
   1977   *The Audubon Society Field Guide to North American Birds.*
          Eastern Region. Alfred A. Knopf, New York, N. Y.
Heintzelman, D. S.
   1979a *A Manual for Bird Watching in the Americas.* Universe Books,
          New York, N. Y.
   1979b *A Guide to Hawk Watching in North America.* Pennsylvania
          State University Press, University Park, Pa.
   1980   *The Illustrated Bird Watcher's Dictionary.* Winchester Press,
          Tulsa, Okla.
Peterson, R. T.
   1961   *A Field Guide to Western Birds.* Second Edition. Houghton
          Mifflin Co., Boston, Mass.
   1980   *A Field Guide to the Birds.* Fourth Edition. Houghton Mifflin
          Co., Boston, Mass.
Pettingill, O. S., Jr.
   1977   *A Guide to Bird Finding East of the Mississippi.* Second Edi-
          tion. Oxford University Press, New York, N. Y.
   1981   *A Guide to Bird Finding West of the Mississippi.* Second
          Edition. Oxford University Press, New York, N. Y.
Robbins, C. S., B. Bruun, H. S. Zim, and A. Singer
   1966   *A Guide to Field Identification/Birds of North America.* Golden
          Press, New York, N. Y.
Udvardy, M. D. F.
   1977   *The Audubon Society Field Guide to North American Birds.*
          Western Region. Alfred A. Knopf, New York, N. Y.

Chapter 2

Enjoying Bird Behavior

Throughout the history of bird watching in North America, primary emphasis was placed on seeing birds in their natural habitats, looking and/or listening to them for relaxation and other recreational reasons, and adding the names of the species observed to a variety of life lists as discussed earlier in *A Manual for Bird Watching in the Americas*. Relatively few recreational birdwatchers made much effort, however, to try to understand the various visual or auditory displays that collectively form much of the basic behavior and language of bird species.

Neglect of bird behavior by birdwatchers was due partly to the fact that they did not know what to look for or how to interpret what they saw. Now that situation is beginning to change. *A Guide to the Behavior of Common Birds* by Donald W. Stokes, introduces birdwatchers to behavior displays used by twenty-five common North American bird species. The author of that book also writes a nontechnical column about bird behavior in the magazine *Bird Watcher's Digest*. Additional technical information of a similar nature is contained in the professional ornithological literature

To most birdwatchers the study of bird behavior is a new and unexplored subject. These nestling Ospreys are attempting to avoid detection.

which most birdwatchers normally don't see but, nevertheless, can consult if they become adequately interested in a particular topic.

To the typical recreational birdwatcher, studying bird behavior is a whole new subject. It is useful, therefore, to discuss the basics of watching bird behavior or avian ethology in nontechnical terms.

BACKGROUND INFORMATION

The behavior of a bird, or any other animal, reflects how it is adapted to its environment, how it makes responses to stimuli in its environment, and what it does in its environment. Although a large variety of concepts and technical terms are used by professional ornithologists when studying bird behavior, recreational birdwatchers first should recognize that the various types of behavior exhibited by an individual bird may be either *maintenance* or *social* behavior. Countless variations of displays are used within each category—which are the two that birdwatchers will want to learn to recognize and separate. Within each the various sequences of movements or actions are known as displays. These can be body movements (called visual displays) or sounds (known as auditory displays).

MAINTENANCE BEHAVIORS

These types of behaviors, as the name suggests, refer to a bird's efforts to maintain its body comfort and care. Thus activities such as hunting, eating, bathing, and selecting suitable habitat and cover are maintenance behaviors. They are important, if not vital, to a bird's daily survival. Thus it is worthwhile to examine the more important types in more detail so that one may begin to recognize and appreciate their functional importance.

Anting is the process by which a bird applies formic acid from ants onto its feathers. The purpose of this avian behavior is not understood completely, but it may destroy feather mites. Some birds engage in active anting during which they use their bills to rub ants against their plumage. Other birds use passive anting in which case ants are allowed to move among the bird's feathers and excrete formic acid onto the feathers. In some instances substitutes for ants—smoke from cigarettes, burning matches, moth balls, and various other species of insects—are used for anting purposes.

Bathing, a common type of bird behavior, also is observed frequently and doubtless would be easily recognized as such by most birdwatchers. In aquatic species such as loons, grebes, cormorants, and waterfowl, one typically sees the birds floating on the water and placing their heads and upper body parts into the water via a scoop-type series of movements. Egrets, herons, and other wading birds typically use a similar form of bathing behavior. Most land birds, including birds of prey, however, fly into a shallow pool or puddle of water, then lower their underparts into the water, and splash water over their bodies. In the case of some special land birds such as swifts, swallows, and hummingbirds, one typically observes them skimming the surface of a water source to take a bath.

Birds also employ a variety of so-called comfort movements many of which are recognized easily by most birdwatchers. Among those to look for are yawning, feather shaking and settling, leg and/or wing stretching, and resting with a bird's head at rest on its shoulders.

Dusting also is used by selected land birds as a means of eliminating external parasites from body or feathers. House Sparrows, for example, fly to dry surface soil and splash the soil over or into their plumage and body much like many land birds engage in bathing. After dusting, the birds then shake their plumage and body vigorously to remove the dust before flying away.

Oiling, a form of behavior in which certain species of birds—especially waterfowl—preen their feathers with oil from the oil gland, also is observed from time to time. The function of oiling is to provide waterproofing to feathers. Generally this is achieved by rubbing oil from the gland onto the bill and then onto the feathers.

Preening probably is the most common, and readily observed, form of maintenance behavior among birds. Most birds preen frequently by running one feather at a time against the partly open bill while assuming varied body postures to facilitate the preening process. It is doubtful that any birdwatcher would not readily recognize preening behavior.

Many people seem to be unaware that birds sleep as do other animals. But sleep they do! In some cases the bird simply turns its head in such a way that it rests on its back or pulls its head into the shoulders.

Sunning is still another pattern of behavior used widely by birds—especially after bathing or dusting, but at other times as well. When sunning, a bird typically spreads its wing and tail feathers and turns in such a way so as to expose as much of its plumage to the sun's rays as possible. Some aquatic birds such as cormorants, and large raptors such as vultures and condors, frequently sun themselves with wings spread while perched on a tree or standing on the ground. The purpose of sunning in some species is not known.

A Canada Goose preening.

SOCIAL BEHAVIORS

Social behaviors are those actions that relate to, or interact with, two or more individuals of the same species or different species. There are a large number of known visual displays of a social nature exhibited by birds—and most species have not yet been studied carefully or at all. However, as far as the needs of recreational birdwatchers are concerned, the basic types of social behavior summarized here are those that are most important to recognize.

Agonistic, or hostile, behavior is not uncommon in one form or another and generally is recognized as such. Threat displays, for example, serve to force an opponent to retreat or escape. Thus a bird defending its nest territory might use threat displays of one type or another to force a rival bird (often a male) to leave the occupied nest territory. The function of threat displays is to produce geographic dispersion of birds and to prevent too many individuals of a given species from living on a particular plot of land. Some birds, of course, are highly colonial in nature and nest in very large colonies but even under those conditions the species recognize tiny territories around their immediate nests and employ agonistic behavior to defend their home ground.

Appeasement displays also are employed commonly by many species of birds to prevent attack and escape. Not infrequently birds sing as part of their agonistic displays. The function of an appeasement display, therefore, is to encourage two birds to come together to form pair bonds for breeding purposes. Thus appeasement displays are quite different in importance and purpose from threat displays.

Defense behavior, also common among birds, is designed to assure the safety and survival among individuals of a species. The object of such behavior may be the preservation of the individual itself or perhaps its young. In any event, birds use a variety of types of defense behavior, the most common and important of which are discussed briefly here.

Not infrequently, especially among perching birds, fleeing and freezing behavior is exhibited in which the bird flies to protective cover and then freezes (remains motionless) until the danger disappears. It is not uncommon also for birds to make vocal warnings or alarm sounds in some circumstances but remain silent under other conditions of danger.

Threat behavior—such as fluffing out the plumage, spreading the wings and tail so the bird looks much larger than normal, and hissing or snapping the bill—also is used in some instances. Nesting birds, however, commonly attack a predator or other source of potential danger if initial use of threats fails to eliminate the danger.

At times some birds also tend to explore or examine closely unfamiliar objects that may appear unexpectedly near nests. The function of such behavior may serve to reveal potential danger to the bird.

Perched hawks and owls that are discovered in exposed locations sometimes are mobbed by flocks of smaller birds. The exact function or purpose of mobbing behavior is not understood fully, but it may be that such activity calls to the attention of birds in a given area the presence of the predators.

A Long-eared Owl's threat display.

During the breeding season, parent birds sometimes use distraction displays to lure predators away from their nests or young. In many instances the parent uses wing and/or body movements that suggest it is injured—called injury-feigning—as an effective means of luring predators away from the nest. The well-known "broken wing act" of the Killdeer is a case in point. Another type of distraction display—called rodent-running because it suggests a rodent running through grass—sometimes is used by birds living among dense ground vegetation such as grass. Such birds tend to sneak away from their nests and then, once at a safe distance, run rapidly with an occasional jump to attract the attention of the predator who is following and actually is being lured farther and farther from the nest and/or young. After the predator is decoyed far from the nest, the parent bird quietly slips away and returns to its nest. I also have observed an aerial version of this sort of rodent-running at Northern Goshawk nests in a forest where the parent birds exposed themselves conspicuously to my presence, lured me away from their nest, then quietly returned to the nest to attend to nesting activities.

Flocking, another aspect of the behavior of some birds, is equally important and interesting to birdwatchers. It can be separated into two major types—colonies and flocks—each seen readily at the correct location and proper season of the year. Both types are important and therefore worthwhile to examine.

Some species of birds—various seabirds, egrets, herons, gulls and terns, swallows and martins, and many tropical blackbirds—nest in groups or colonies of varying size, some extraordinarily large. Within such colonies, however, each pair of breeding birds maintains a small nest territory—often not larger than the maximum distance a bird on its nest can reach with its bill. Visits to bird colonies (always no closer than the outer edge of the colony) whether Adelie or King Penguins in the Antarctic, gulls or terns along one of our coastlines, or seabirds such as Northern Gannets on Bonaventure Island, Quebec, always are bird-watching highlights because of their aesthetic appeal and because of opportunities to study activities of large numbers of birds with ease. Many different aspects of colonial bird behavior can be identified within a colony within a short period of time, thus making it easy to grasp and appreciate the broad spectrum of behavior patterns of a given species on-the-spot.

Many species of birds also form flocks, sometimes of considerable size, other than during the breeding season. Such flocks generally contain individuals of the same species, but sometimes (as among blackbirds) flocks of mixed species of the same size and flight speeds develop. Thus, during autumn, I often observe mixed flocks of Red-winged Blackbirds and Common Grackles at some of the hawk migration lookouts in the eastern Pennsylvania mountains. Probably the most widely seen examples of flocking behavior, however, are the spring and autumn migrations of Canada Geese, Snow Geese, Whistling Swans, Broad-winged Hawks, and Sandhill Cranes that cross the skies of portions of North America. Sometimes many hundreds of individuals form such flocks (occasionally a thousand or more birds in the case of the hawks), thus providing birdwatchers with fascinating and spectacular attractions to observe and study. Counting migrating hawks also is fascinating. Indeed, thousands of people now occupy many

A colony of nesting Northern Gannets on Bonaventure Island, Quebec.

happy days in spring and autumn engaged in such worthwhile outdoor activities. Sometimes such efforts even produce information new to ornithological science.

Regardless of the size and type of organization, flocking by birds serves several important purposes including better prospects of locating and using food and less possibility of suffering damage or death by predators. In some species it also may help to maintain rough family units outside of the breeding season. On the other hand, as in the case of many hawks forming flocks or "kettles" inside thermals, formation of the flock may reflect nothing more than birds using the thermal to aid them in flight.

NESTING BEHAVIOR

A variety of behavior types also are used by birds as they engage in nesting activities. Some already have been touched upon. Oth-

A flock of Snow Geese.

ers are occasional or daily activities used to maintain successful nesting. Some of these types of nesting behavior offer birdwatchers opportunities to engage in projects that might not only serve to educate the birders working on the projects, but also may produce new scientific information previously unknown to ornithologists.

Defense of nest territory is one aspect of nesting behavior that can serve as the subject of a birdwatcher's study. Do both sexes of a nesting pair of birds defend their territory? In some instances, such as American Kestrels, Northern Cardinals, and various other species, sex can be easily recognized among individual birds. Then it is relatively easy to make careful observations of the activities of the birds in the vicinity of their nests to determine the roles of the two sexes in nest territory defense. But in other instances, where little or no external difference in pattern and/or coloration of plumage is obvious between the sexes, advanced techniques are necessary to determine which bird is the male, and the other the female, and these techniques are beyond the scope of most birdwatchers' training and experience.

Determining the size of a bird's nest territory also is a project that can be worthwhile. Birdwatchers should be able to engage in this sort of project without undue difficulty. One first maps the area in the general vicinity of the bird's nest, showing buildings, vegetation, and other objects in their proper positions. Then mark on the map the locations where the nesting birds stop when they sing, display, or otherwise exhibit clear indications of territorial defense. Eventually enough of these marks will show the outermost points of the nest territory used by the birds. One can then draw lines between the outermost points on the map to see a relatively accurate outline of the size and shape of the nest territory. This project can be done easily for nesting American Robins, or other common species, either in one's backyard or an entire neighborhood.

The process of nest building also offers birdwatchers opportunities to study and gather other details about the behavior activities of birds. One can, for example, determine the roles of the two sexes in nest building, document cooperative types of behavior between the pair, and accurately time the duration of activities of the two birds to determine the relative time budget of

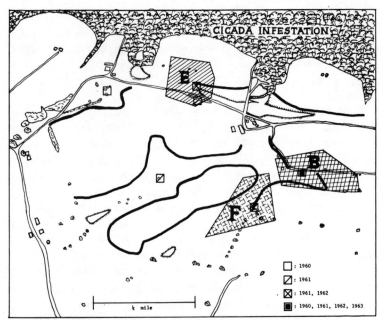

American Kestrel nest territories on an eastern Pennsylvania farm. Reprinted from Heintzelman (1964) in the Wilson Bulletin.

the birds in the nest building process. Or, birdwatchers can record the types of supporting structure common species of birds use to build their nests. Do American Robins, for example, select specific types of trees or other structures more regularly than others? How high are nests of Northern Orioles placed above the ground? What is the range and average height of oriole nests above the ground? Is one type of tree favored by orioles over another in which to build their nests? These are typical questions that can develop into birdwatcher projects when birds are nesting.

As soon as breeding birds lay eggs in their nests, various project opportunities are available. For example, do both sexes incubate the eggs? Or, does the female do all of the incubation? If so, what is the role of the male while his mate is incubating? How many eggs are deposited to form a complete clutch? If the eggs are numbered *very lightly* with a soft lead pencil, as they appear in the nest, what is the time of incubation (in days or hours) of each marked egg? Relatively little information is available on the incubation time of marked bird eggs, but to engage in this sort of study it may be necessary to secure special permits from state and federal wildlife officials *before* work is begun.

After the eggs hatch, do both parents feed the nestlings? How often? What are the birds fed? Which parents remove fecal sacs in species which produce them? What is the rate of growth and weight of the nestlings during their nestling period?

Clearly an endless series of questions can be asked, and developed into projects for curious birdwatchers interested in the nesting behavior of birds. Some projects are simple, but others require long hours, days, or weeks of careful observation and record keeping before answers are obtained. How much time and effort a birdwatcher puts into a project is dependent upon the goals and enthusiasm of each person. Nevertheless, the opportunities are there for birdwatcher projects—either informally as

A Gray Catbird removing a fecal sac from a nestling.

discussed here or more formally as in life history studies discussed next.

LIFE HISTORY STUDIES

Amateur birdwatchers should never think that they can't conduct worthwhile studies or other projects with birds. That is particularly true of life history studies. Perhaps the finest and most comprehensive life history study ever conducted of a single species was done on the Song Sparrow by an amateur ornithologist (but professionally trained zoologist) in her backyard. As a result, Margaret Morse Nice was one of the most respected and leading students of bird behavior in the world. Her classic *Studies in the Life History of the Song Sparrow* is a model upon which many of today's students can pattern their own work.

Equally important were the monumental 23 volumes of Arthur Cleveland Bent's *Life Histories of North American Birds* published by the Smithsonian Institution (reprinted by Dover Publications) between 1919 and 1968. Bent was not a professional

A nesting Song Sparrow.

ornithologist, but his determination in gathering all available worthwhile information about North American birds resulted in a basic collection of life history information that even today serves as the first reference upon which new studies are built. In short, he created an ornithological monument! Unlike many branches of science, ornithology and bird watching have always been served well by qualified amateurs and it is likely that this trend will continue well into the future. Indeed, the important role of the amateur in bird watching and ornithology now is a well established tradition.

Birdwatchers seriously considering conducting a life history study of a particular species—even common species need such studies—should understand that this type of project requires extremely careful and accurate attention to detail, as well as extended periods of time both in gathering the field data and in writing the results of the field study for publication in ornithological journals. People who are not prepared to devote the time and energy necessary for completion of such work would best restrict their efforts to isolated aspects of a bird's life history. But those people who enjoy uncovering new information and expanding knowledge of wildlife can use the outline in the appendix as a basis for establishing the types of questions that need to be asked and answered when studying a bird's life history.

ADDITIONAL READING

Armstrong, E. A.
    1947 *Bird Display and Behavior*. Revised Edition. Lindsay Drummond, London.
Bent, A. C.
    1919 *Life Histories of North American Birds*. Smithsonian Institu-
    –68 tion, Washington, D. C. Reprinted by Dover Publications, New York, N. Y.
Berger, A. J.
    1961 *Bird Study*. Dover Publications, Inc., New York, N. Y. (Chapter 5).
Burton, M.
    1959 *Phoenix Re-born*. Hutchinson Publishing Group, Ltd., London.
Dilger, W. C.
    1962 Methods and Objectives of Ethology. *Living Bird*, 1: 83–92.
Emlen, J. T., Jr.

1955 The Study of Behavior in Birds. In *Recent Studies in Avian Biology,* University of Illinois Press, Urbana, Ill.

Farner, D. S. and J. R. King
1971 *Avian Biology.* Volume one. Academic Press, New York, N. Y. (Chapter 11).

Ficken, M. S. and R. W. Ficken
1962 The Comparative Ethology of the Wood Warblers. *Living Bird,* 1: 103–122.

Hartshorne, C.
1973 *Born to Sing: An Interpretation and World Survey of Bird Song.* Indiana University Press, Bloomington, Ind.

Heintzelman, D. S.
1975 *Autumn Hawk Flights: The Migrations in Eastern North America.* Rutgers University Press, New Brunswick, N. J.
1979 *A Guide to Hawk Watching in North America.* Pennsylvania State University Press, University Park, Pa.

Howard, E.
1948 *Territory in Bird Life.* Collins, London.

Johnsgard, P. A.
1965 *Handbook of Waterfowl Behavior.* Cornell University Press, Ithaca, N. Y.

Lack, D.
1947 *Darwin's Finches.* University Press, Cambridge.

Lorenz, K.
1952 *King Solomon's Ring.* Thomas Y. Crowell, New York, N. Y.
1979 *The Year of the Greylag Goose.* Harcourt Brace Jovanovich, Inc., New York, N. Y.

Nice, M. M.
1962 Development of Behavior in Precocial Birds. *Trans. Linnaean Society New York,* 8: 1–211.
1964 *Studies in the Life History of the Song Sparrow.* Volume 2. Dover Publications, New York, N. Y.

Pettingill, O. S., Jr.
1967 *Ornithology in Laboratory and Field.* Fourth Ed. Burgess Publishing Co., Minneapolis, Minn.
1975 *Another Penguin Summer.* Charles Scribner's Sons, New York, N. Y.

Penney, R. L.
1968 Territorial and Social Behavior in the Adelie Penguin. *Antarctic Research Ser.,* 12: 83–131.

Peterson, R. T.
1979 *Penguins.* Houghton Mifflin Co., Boston, Mass.

Snow, D. W.
1976 *The Web of Adaptation. Bird Studies in the American Tropics.* William Collins Sons & Co., Ltd., London.

Stokes, D. W.
  1979 *A Guide to the Behavior of Common Birds.* Little, Brown and Co., Boston, Mass.
Thomson, A. L. (Ed.).
  1964 *A New Dictionary of Birds.* McGraw-Hill Book Co., New York, N. Y.
Thorpe, W. H.
  1961 *Bird-Song: The Biology of Vocal Communication and Expression in Birds.* University Press, Cambridge.
Tinbergen, N.
  1960 *The Herring Gull's World.* Basic Books, Inc., New York, N. Y.
  1965 *Animal Behavior.* Time-Life Books, New York, N. Y.
Welty, J. C.
  1962 *The Life of Birds.* W. B. Saunders Co., Philadelphia, Pa. (Chapter 9).

Chapter 3

The Birdwatcher and Ecological Isolation

Few birdwatchers think of themselves as ecologists, yet most gradually develop an awareness of some basic ecological principles. Two are particularly important. They are habitat and ecological niche. Both can result in ecological isolation among birds and thus species survival. Therefore it is important to consider each and try to understand each when participating in recreational bird watching, because a fuller and richer appreciation of birds and their evolution and survival will result.

HABITAT AND GEOGRAPHY

The importance of learning the habitat requirements for various species is obvious and necessary if one is to locate particular species of birds effectively. One would not search for a nesting Olive-sided Flycatcher, for example, on the marshes of New Jersey's Brigantine National Wildlife Refuge. But an excursion to the state's salt meadows would be appropriate to see nesting

Laughing Gulls. These, of course, are broad examples of habitat
separation and isolation. A far more rewarding activity is to examine habitat isolation among congeneric species—birds classified in the same genus. They are species that are evolutionary
relatives, yet sufficiently different to require different habitats
and/or ecological niches.

The three North American hawks in the genus *Accipiter*—
Northern Goshawk, Sharp-shinned Hawk, and Cooper's Hawk—
are not only generally separated from each other by habitat but
also by sexual size and food habits, thus resulting in six ecologically separated forms. The largest, the Northern Goshawk, generally selects large forests and extensive woodlands in which to
nest, whereas the species of intermediate size, the Cooper's Hawk,
prefers wooded areas, large woodlots, canyons, and riverine
woodland for nest habitat. Finally the small Sharp-shinned Hawk
also nests in forests and woodland but it occupies an ecological
niche separate from the Northern Goshawk.

In all three accipiters, however, the females are about one-third
larger than the males. This results in somewhat different prey
being taken by each sex and each species for a total of six different
general prey groups. Sharp-shinned Hawks tend to concentrate
on smaller birds such as wood warblers, whereas Cooper's Hawks
prefer larger birds such as Common Flickers, American Robins,
European Starlings, Eastern Meadowlarks, and Common Grackles. The larger and more powerful Northern Goshawk, however,
tends to capture large- and medium-size mammals and birds such
as Red Squirrels and American Crows. Thus ecological isolation
of the three species of hawks is achieved by habitat separation
and niche isolation. The final result is a more even geographic
and ecological distribution of predation upon other wildlife species and food supply for the predators.

In the forests of the Central Appalachians one finds Red-tailed
Hawks, Red-shouldered Hawks, and Broad-winged Hawks—three
species classified in the genus *Buteo,* plus the Cooper's Hawk
which is a member of the genus *Accipiter*—all nesting in the same
areas. Until recently, however, the ecological factors responsible
for allowing these species to co-exist in the same areas were
unknown. Recent field studies by Kimberly Titus and James Mosher
now provide some fascinating explanations and insights into the

Wetland habitat.

factors responsible for allowing the use of these forests by these predators.

To begin, each species tends to select specific areas in which to construct its nest—areas avoided as nest sites by the other forest-living species. The Red-tailed Hawk, for example, tends to nest higher in trees than do either the Red-shouldered Hawk or Broad-winged Hawk and to locate its nest on steep slopes close to the top of ridges far from forest openings or water. Moreover, there generally tends to be a lack of obstructions on the downslope side of the nests which gives the hawks direct access to their nests. In comparison, Red-shouldered Hawks tend to nest near water and to use large trees in mature, moist forests. Red-shoulder nests also are constructed much farther below the forest canopy top than are nests of Red-tailed Hawks. Broad-winged Hawks generally nest quite close to water and put their nests in trees close to openings in the forest. Finally, the Cooper's Hawks tend to select nest sites somewhat higher in trees than are used by either Red-shouldered or Broad-winged Hawks, and the birds also prefer locations with heavily grown understory and ground cover in mature forests. Thus the situation in the Central Appalachians shows that subtle, but important, differences in habitat types tend to become a factor in the ecological isolation of these four birds of prey even though they can live in the same forests. Probably food habitat differences play additional roles in helping to isolate the various species.

In a similar manner, two resident species of eagles in North America—Golden Eagles and Bald Eagles—also are ecologically isolated from each other during most of the year because of differences in preference in nesting habitat as well as food habits. Golden Eagles are generally mountain birds (even in the East where a small Appalachian population persists) which feed upon rabbits and similar mammalian prey. In comparison, Bald Eagles are aquatic birds that usually nest in locations close to water (a few also nest in desert locations in the Southwest) and feed largely upon fish. Only during migration in spring and autumn do the two species generally tend to come into close contact with each other (a few also may do so in winter), and even then little interaction seems to occur between the species.

Finally, the nesting falcons of North America north of Mexico provide still another example of related species being ecologically isolated both by habitat, geography, and food habits. The largest species in the genus, the Gyrfalcon, is an Arctic bird which has no competition for nest sites from other falcons except perhaps some Arctic Peregrine Falcons. However, Gyrfalcons tend to capture birds that are permanent Arctic residents, whereas Peregrines tend to use migrating birds as their main source of food. For the most part, however, Gyrfalcons tend to occupy foothill tundra as well as alpine areas. In such areas, they can nest in a variety of locations including sea cliffs, river bluffs, and other cliffs on escarpments removed from water but which tend to be less accessible than are cliffs used by Arctic-nesting Peregrine Falcons. In comparison, breeding Peregrines of the North American Arctic occupy both taiga and tundra zones, but almost always select sea cliffs on the mainland or on islands, or cliffs on river bluffs beside running waterways in the interior. Most of these nests tend to be more accessible than are Peregrine nests farther south in North America.

In southern Canada and much of the Northeast, where Gyrfalcons do not occur as breeding birds, Peregrine Falcons tend to have rather rigid nest site requirements. Along one section of the Hudson River in the Palisades Interstate Park, four major factors are known to govern successful Peregrine nesting, after one considers the basic requirement of a mountain craig or cliff overlooking a river. First, the location must contain suitable ledges for nesting, perching, and feeding. Second, there can be no large trees which might tend to block flight or visibility. Third, the Peregrine cliffs must be long and contain several ledges instead of only one narrow ledge. Finally the site must prevent disturbance from above.

Because such sites are rather selective, many Peregrine Falcon cliffs had very long histories of occupancy involving generations of birds. In 1942, for example, ornithologist Joseph J. Hickey documented the locations of 408 sites east of the Rockies, many used for decades. He estimated that this number represented about an 11 percent decline compared with the Peregrine Falcon's original population level.

In comparison with the nesting requirements of Peregrines, Prairie Falcons of the western United States occupy the lower

Peregrine Falcons are famous for selecting cliffs near rivers as nest sites.

foothills and plains not necessarily associated with rivers. In such areas canyons, bluffs, and cliffs serve as nest sites and from them they often visit winter wheat-growing areas on gently rolling farmland where Horned Larks occur in considerable numbers. These larks form one major food item in the diet of this inland falcon, although other birds and mammals also are taken as prey items.

The Merlin, one of the smaller North American falcons, breeds in taiga, prairie-parkland areas, and humid coastal forests of the Pacific coast where nests are placed in heavily forested areas containing many lakes and exposed areas. In some locations, mixed second-growth forest in close proximity to water also serves as nest sites, and some Merlins even nest in trees in urban settings in parts of southern Canada. Nevertheless, none of these habitat types compares with the requirements of other North American falcons and the birds, therefore, do not compete for nesting sites with any other North American falcons.

Finally the American Kestrel, the smallest of the North American falcons, is a bird of open agricultural or other country. It nests either in natural cavities in trees, nest boxes provided for that purpose, or similar locations. Much of its diet consists of small rodents and insects. It, too, does not compete for habitat or food needed by any other North American falcon and therefore is ecologically isolated from its other continental relatives.

The nuthatches in the genus *Sitta* provide another example of habitat isolation, and some niche isolation, among species of birds of the same genus. Although the genus has representatives throughout the world, four species occur in North America: White-breasted Nuthatch, Red-breasted Nuthatch, Brown-headed Nuthatch, and Pygmy Nuthatch. How, then, are these birds separated from each other?

The White-breasted Nuthatch is the largest of the four and nests mainly in broad-leaved woodland or pineland south of the range of the Red-breasted Nuthatch. On the other hand, the Brown-headed Nuthatch is a bird of the pine forests of the Southeast. Finally the Pygmy Nuthatch lives in the Yellow Pine forests of the Pacific coast and other western forests. Since it is smaller than the White-breasted Nuthatch, which occurs in the same habitat, it obtains food high in trees from needles and cones rather than the large limbs and trunks preferred by White-breasted Nuthatches.

There are, of course, other examples that could be given to illustrate habitat isolation among birds of the same genus but those provided are adequate to illustrate the idea. But what about ecological niche requirements?

NICHE

Within a given habitat, two species can live together only if they occupy different ecological niches. This, stated formally, is the principle of competitive exclusion. That is, two species living together do not carry out *exactly* the same activities in exactly the same habitat or direct competition would result and one would be eliminated from that particular niche or habitat.

How, then, can a knowledge of niche requirements aid a birdwatcher in deriving more enjoyment from the hobby? One way is by allowing the person to understand better the workings of food chains and food webs. Let's consider some examples, using first the foraging range of wood warblers. Not all warblers seek food in the same locations within their required breeding habitats. Some search for food close to the ground, others at medium heights, and still others at the top of tall vegetation. In other words, the ecological niches of the various species are distributed in layers, or stratified, according to the various heights which vegetation attains. Examples of warblers with foraging ranges confined to the lower vegetative strata are: Canada, Kentucky, Prairie, and Worm-eating. Species with medium foraging ranges include Black-and-White, Black-throated Blue, Golden-winged, Blue-winged, and Magnolia. Some high foraging species are Blackburnian and Cerulean. However, not all warblers are rigidly restricted to specific strata in conducting their foraging activities. Chestnut-sided and Hooded Warblers, range from low to medium levels; but Nashville and Yellow Warblers move from medium to low ranges. And the Black-throated Green Warbler ranges from medium to high levels in its food-gathering efforts. The Cape May Warbler sometimes ranges from high to medium levels.

Other factors which also permit utilization of different ecological niches are differences in a species' anatomy or morphology. Among herons and egrets, for example, the Great Blue Heron is able to exploit food sources in deep water because of its long legs. Common Egrets would seek food in shallower water, and Black-crowned Night Herons would confine their feeding efforts to the shallowest water of all. Hence, in these examples, the physical size of the various species determines more or less where each can feed.

Similarly, the woodpeckers of North America have evolved into two branches each leading to increased specialization. The unspecialized flickers (*Colaptes*) form the base from which the two woodpecker branches are derived. On one side, the Pileated Woodpecker remains relatively primitive and more or less resorts to behavior and ecological niche affinities similar to flickers. But at the apex of this branch appears the rigidly specialized Ivory-billed Woodpecker whose niche requirements are so specific that the species is nearly extinct (if it is not already so) due to loss of most of its required habitat. (Alternative habitats do not meet its niche requirements.)

The other branch of the woodpeckers' evolutionary tree contains species such as the Hairy Woodpecker, whose niche centers upon tree trunks and large limbs, and the nearly identical but proportionally smaller Downy Woodpecker, which occupies a niche on smaller branches and twigs. The Yellow-bellied Sapsucker has a specialized tongue with a brush-like tip, thus enabling it to feed effectively on sap oozing from holes it drills in trees. Finally, at the top of the evolutionary branch one finds the peculiar three-toed woodpeckers. Of course, not all these woodpecker species occupy the same habitats. Some species are distributionally separated.

The fruit-eating behavior of tanagers in Trinidad's mountainous Northern Range offers additional examples of niche exploitation and its role in governing bird distribution within a given habitat. Of the island's three attractive *Tangara* species, the Speckled Tanager is mainly a forest-dwelling bird. While remaining in a perched position, it picks fruit and eats it whole. The Bay-headed Tanager also eats fruit, but it pecks pieces and sometimes while airborne in manakin-fashion takes fruit. Finally, the Turquoise Tanager often is found in flocks. This species also perches to pick fruit and seems prone to pick pieces of large fruits. Turquoise Tanagers also mandibulate fruit in an apparent effort to reduce its size or eliminate seeds before swallowing it. Mistletoe fruit forms a larger proportion of this tanager's diet than in other species.

In the American tropics there also are five species of kingfishers that range in size from the large Ringed Kingfisher, similar in appearance to the Belted Kingfisher of North America, to the tiny Pygmy Kingfisher. To some extent these neotropical kingfishers occupy different habitats and thus do not compete with each other for food. For example, the Ringed Kingfisher catches fish in open, deeper streams whereas the tiny Pygmy Kingfisher often consumes insects captured along small streams running through tropical forest. But along many of the small rivers and streams running into the Amazon River I have sometimes observed at least three kingfisher species—Ringed, Amazon, and Green—along the same small waterway. It is not at all clear what niches these species occupy when they occur in the same habitat, yet there must be differences in niche requirements between them.

One final example of ecological niche separation can be presented, this time from the central Galapagos islands off the coast of Ecuador. One finds on these central islands five species of

Galapagos ground finches in the genus *Geospiza*. Four of these five species also live in the coastal arid zones of the islands. Thus they occupy much the same type of habitat. Careful study, however, demonstrates that each of the four also occupies a different ecological niche and therefore does not compete with the ground finches with which it associates. The Cactus Finch, for example, feeds mostly on fruits and flowers of *Opuntia* cactus—food upon which the other three ground finches in the arid zones do not feed. Indeed, in those sections of the central islands where *Opuntia* does not grow the Cactus Finch also is absent.

The remaining three arid zone ground finches, however, use different types of food. The Small Ground Finch, for example, has a small and narrow bill and eats mostly soft, small seeds. The somewhat larger Medium Ground Finch, on the other hand, feeds mainly on harder and larger seeds, and the even larger Large Ground Finch is known to select a higher proportion of harder and larger seeds than the Medium Ground Finch prefers. Thus, for the most part, these four arid zone ground finches of the central Galapagos islands occupy different ecological niches and can therefore live together in the same habitat.

These examples deal only with a few aspects of the complex subject of niche requirements of birds. Many important additional factors can be involved in determining a bird's niche requirements. Nevertheless, even cursory observations of niche requirements offer curious birdwatchers an opportunity to derive added pleasure from their hobby. Why merely look at a bird when you can attempt to understand its ecological role? So sharpen your observational skills, and ask yourself probing questions regarding the activities of the birds you see. You may discover something new to science as well as enhance the rewards derived from your bird-watching activities.

One project in which birdwatchers can engage is a simple analysis of ecological isolation of a given area such as a park, island, isolated mountain range, or other geographic feature. Start such a project during the breeding season by listing all species of birds living on the area. After this preliminary list is prepared, determine the genus of each species by reference to the American Ornithologists' Union's *Check-List of North American Birds*

(available in most natural history museums, some college libraries, and most college biology departments that offer ornithology
courses), the American Birding Association's *A.B.A. Checklist:
Birds of Continental United States and Canada,* or perhaps recently published field guides to North American birds.

The purpose of making the list is to determine which breeding
species on the area are congeneric (placed in the same genus) and
thus to establish the presence of closely related birds that might
have similar living requirements and therefore tend to compete
with each other for food, cover, nest sites, or other survival needs.
If, for example, two or more species of thrushes nest in the area
being studied, and the thrushes are closely related to each other,
one can try to determine what ecological factors are different and
unique to each species in its life history. This could be different
elevations being used on a mountain, slightly different nest site
requirements, different foraging areas in which the birds hunt for
food, or any number of other subtle but important factors that
would tend to separate one species from the other in the study
area. Preparation of an accurate map showing the exact locations
of all nests of the various species might reveal isolation among
some birds as far as nest locations are concerned. One can then
either check each nest location to determine what differences
might be obvious—especially in nests that are isolated from the
others—or perhaps overlay the nest site location map on top of
an accurate vegetation-type map of the same area to determine
if different vegetation types seem to be an ecological isolating
factor.

There will be many times, of course, when it is not possible to
determine what ecological isolation factors are working in a particular area. But in some instances simple, but careful, observation might reveal previously unsuspected (perhaps even unknown) factors of considerable scientific interest and importance.
For the purpose of most birdwatchers, however, it is unnecessary
to try to engage in very complex or costly research projects to
enjoy exploring the subject of ecological isolation among birds.

A variety of background information is published on this subject, and some are listed at the end of this chapter. David Lack's
Ecological Isolation in Birds is particularly readable and helpful,

and a source of excellent ideas and examples of how scientists study ecological isolation among birds. It is recommended highly to all birdwatchers interested in this subject.

ADDITIONAL READING

Allen, G. M.
    1962   *Birds and their Attributes*. Dover Publications, Inc., New York, N. Y.
Cade, T. J.
    1960   Ecology of the Peregrine and Gyrfalcon Populations in Alaska. *Univ. Calif. Pubs. Zoology,* 63 (3): 151–290.
Farner, D. S. and J. R. King
    1971   *Avian Biology*. Volume one. Academic Press, New York, N. Y.
Griscom, L. and A. Sprunt, Jr.
    1957   *The Warblers of America*. Devin-Adair Co., New York, N. Y.
Harris, M.
    1974   *A Field Guide to the Birds of Galapagos*. Taplinger Publishing Co., New York, N. Y.
Heintzelman, D. S.
    1973   The Birder and Ecological Niche. *New Jersey Nature News,* 28 (2): 68–70.
    1979   *Hawks and Owls of North America*. Universe Books, New York, N. Y.
Lack, D.
    1971   *Ecological Isolation in Birds*. Harvard University Press, Cambridge, Mass.
Snow, D. W.
    1976   *The Web of Adaptation*. William Collins Sons & Co., Ltd., London.
Snow, B. K. and D. W. Snow
    1971   The Feeding Ecology of Tanagers and Honeycreepers in Trinidad. *Auk,* 88: 291–322.
Titus, K. and J. A. Mosher
    1981   Nest-Site Habitat Selected by Woodland Hawks in the Central Appalachians. *Auk,* 98 (2): 270–281.

Chapter 4

Locality Bird Watching

During the early years of the Age of Bird Watching, birders generally confined their field efforts to local areas near their homes such as studying the birds in one's home county. Sometimes bird watching was even restricted to one town, the area around a particular lake, or the birds observed migrating past one particular hawk migration lookout. Great emphasis was placed on exploring such local areas on foot, slowly and repeatedly, during many years, while searching every possible haunt in which birds might occur. The result of such careful bird-watching efforts was the accumulation of accurate and comprehensive records of the birdlife (and its subtle changes) of one locality.

More recently, however, with the advent of Interstate and other excellent highways, an abundance of automobiles, jet airplanes, and an increasing desire to develop huge life lists among the "listing" segment of the bird-watching community, the trend in part of the birding community in the United States shifted toward venturing farther from home to find birds in less familiar places. Indeed, some birdwatchers became jet set bird listers! Perhaps the most celebrated of these listing efforts is that of James M. Vardaman who observed 699 species of birds in 1979 in North America and described his unique and costly project in *Call Collect, Ask For Birdman*.

With soaring energy and other travel expenses, however, many young or newer birdwatchers again are discovering the value and enjoyment available in local—so-called locality—bird watching so familiar to birders with long experience. It seems useful, therefore, to examine several examples of locality bird watching because they illustrate nicely the benefits of such local efforts. First, however, it is desirable to present some general hints for engaging in locality bird watching.

WHAT TO INCLUDE IN LOCALITY BIRD LISTS

Proper preparation of locality bird lists for publication depends entirely upon solid, accurate bird records from the area being studied. These records can take various forms. First, one can use valid sight observations provided they are made by capable observers who are not afraid to admit that they can't identify all the birds they see and thus willingly reject those records which are in doubt. All records, however, should receive critical evaluation at the time they are made and perhaps later as well. Second, one also should use and refer to preserved specimens in museum collections if the skins contain basic label information, such as date and location obtained. Egg collections and nest record cards also contain important information.

Next, good photographic records of rare birds—when they clearly show vital field marks of the species—should be cited and/or reproduced.

Finally, records published in the ornithological and bird-watching literature also should be used after critical evaluation of such records. As a result of using all of these records, one should be able to produce an accurate and worthwhile accounting of the birdlife of one's geographic area of interest.

A Maine Study

Coastal Maine is certainly one of the world's most beautiful natural areas, and one of the most beloved sections of the rocky

Maine coastline is the Penobscot Bay area. So it is not unexpected that careful field studies have been made of various sections of Maine including the water and land birds of the Penobscot Bay area. These investigations were conducted by Frederick V. Hebard and published in 1959 and 1960 under the titles *Water Birds of Penobscot Bay* and *The Land Birds of Penobscot Bay* by the Portland Society of Natural History.

Using both previously published ornithological records for the area, as well as his own field observations, Hebard produced a valuable summary of the past and present status of the bay area's birdlife including the status of such fascinating and delightful species as the Common Eider, Arctic Tern, Razorbill, and Atlantic Puffin. Despite the charm of these and other waterbirds, landbirds such as wood warblers also are of exceptional interest to birdwatchers because of the large variety of species that nest in the Penobscot Bay area. In addition, the area also is an important spring and autumn migration route for many small landbirds, raptors such as Sharp-shinned Hawks, and other species. Frederick Hebard's work provides documentation and a solid reference for future birdwatchers visiting or living in the area and the basis upon which new studies in the future can be built.

A Massachusetts Study

By any unit of measure, Massachusetts is one of the most active and leading centers of bird watching and ornithological study in North America. Organizations such as the Massachusetts Audubon Society and the Nuttall Ornithological Club, both based in the state, have played major roles in regional, state, national, and international affairs. In addition, this state produced one of the finest state bird books ever published in terms of scientific information, literary merit, and artistic illustrations—Edward Howe Forbush's monumental three volume *Birds of Massachusetts and Other New England States* with magnificent color illustrations painted by the master of bird artists Louis Agassiz Fuertes.

Against such an illustrious background, it would seem difficult if not impossible to produce a regional work of equal importance. Yet just such a magnificent work was written and published by Aaron Clark Bagg and Samuel Atkins Eliot, Jr. in the form of their massive 813-page book *Birds of the Connecticut Valley in Massachusetts* published in 1937. Covering a square about 50 miles on a side, the book details in extraordinary depth the past and present status of the birds of the Connecticut Valley using all available past, present, and worthwhile unpublished information. In all, 301 species are treated in the volume including such extinct birds as the Heath Hen and Passenger Pigeon. Some of the information included extends back as far as one hundred years. A particularly important feature of the book is the authors' extremely critical acceptance or rejection of records. Thus the finished result represents as accurate and correct a picture of past and changing present birdlife of the Connecticut Valley as is possible to produce. Moreover, an unshakably solid foundation is provided for all future studies of the same area—for which future birdwatchers and ornithologists should forever be grateful. Few areas of the United States can boast such important and invaluable comparative material.

Adding to the value of the book are numerous black-and-white photographs showing birds of particular interest to the area. However, the centerpiece of the book's illustrations is the magnificent painting of a Peregrine Falcon by Louis Agassiz Fuertes reproduced in full color. Some consider the painting the finest bird portrait Fuertes ever completed. It is a classic in bird art and adds the final stamp of approval to a book that stands as a monument in American ornithology.

Some Pennsylvania Studies

Pennsylvania, with its many habitats and rich birdlife, is a splendid place to enjoy bird watching. Thus it is hardly surprising that it produced many outstanding ornithologists and birdwatchers during its long history. Some made studies of the birds of several counties so that today we have detailed records of the past status of birds in those areas. Three examples out of the many from which one could select come to mind immediately.

In the heart of the delightful Pennsylvania German section of the eastern part of the state one finds Lancaster County. It was there, in 1924, that Herbert H. Beck—a well-known amateur birdwatcher and naturalist, and a professor at Franklin and Marshall

College, published *A Chapter on the Ornithology of Lancaster County, Pennsylvania* containing a wealth of historical bird records augmented by more than 35 years of his own bird observations in the county. The book also records the Pennsylvania German bird names used by the citizens of the county thus adding to the overall value of the work. Of more than minor interest were historical records of nesting Golden Eagles and past reports of extinct species such as Passenger Pigeon and Carolina Parakeet.

Not far away, in Cumberland County, an equally rich heritage of bird watching began in 1845 when Spencer F. Baird published a catalog of birds he recorded in the vicinity of Carlisle, Pennsylvania. Baird later became a Secretary of the Smithsonian Institution and a celebrated American ornithologist. A century later, in 1943, a minister and birdwatcher, Edward Snively Frey, published *The Centennial Check-List of the Birds of Cumberland County, Pennsylvania and Her Borders* in which he compiled all current and historical bird records for the county and compared them with Baird's list produced a century earlier. The result was a fascinating accounting of more than 100 years of changes in the birdlife of Cumberland County. One of the facts revealed was that Baird apparently knew nothing of the spectacular autumn hawk migrations that occur annually along the Kittatinny Ridge only a few miles north of Carlisle. Today hawk watchers enjoy these migrations from lookouts at Waggoner's Gap and occasionally Sterretts Gap. One wishes, however, that Baird would have studied the raptor migrations and made seasonal counts of the various species so that today we might have a historical base against which to compare variations in the hawk counts we make today.

Berks County also is located deep within Pennsylvania German country. It, too, has a rich heritage of bird study because of the efforts of Earl L. Poole and a host of other birdwatchers. Indeed, Poole's *A Half Century of Bird Life in Berks County, Pennsylvania* presents a comprehensive picture of the birds of the county documented with exceptional and critical care—a model of how a county bird list can be published. Among the important data included in the book are numerous shorebird records, and other aquatic species, seen at Lake Ontelaunee near the city of Reading. Adding charm and value to the book, too, are numerous pen-and-ink sketches of birds drawn by Dr. Poole, who was a bird and mammal artist of wide recognition. Generations of future birdwatchers in Berks County thus have a solid foundation upon which to compare future trends in their local birdlife. They owe Dr. Poole an incomparable debt of gratitude for his decades of devotion to Berks County bird study.

In the northeastern section of Pennsylvania, the Pocono Mountains extend over a plateau rising in elevation between 1,600 and more than 2,000 feet above mean sea level. Despite extensive development, especially within recent years, much of the area still remains forested and reflects a notable northern flavor. Since the beginning of American ornithology, the Poconos have been of considerable interest to ornithologists and later birdwatchers. In 1804, Alexander Wilson (the father of American ornithology) passed through the region and collected the specimen of the White-winged Crossbill and the White-crowned Sparrow included in the plates of his *American Ornithology*. In 1829, John James Audubon also visited the Pocono region and remained there for six weeks, making many drawings. Then followed a long line of bird students which, from about 1893 and the explorations of the recently formed Delaware Valley Ornithological Club of Philadelphia, have continued to the present. Certainly during this century the DVOC and its members have played a major role in documenting the birdlife of the Poconos. In 1956, this culminated with the publication by Phillips B. Street of *Birds of the Pocono Mountains, Pennsylvania* and in 1975 of an update entitled *Birds of the Pocono Mountains, 1955–1975*. When combined, these two publications form the major record of the birds of this section of Pennsylvania and stand as an outstanding example of the type of work that can result from decades of careful study of a particular region of a state.

Of all Pennsylvania geographic bird studies, however, the one that remains monumental in its scope and depth of coverage is W. E. Clyde Todd's *Birds of Western Pennsylvania*. This magnificent 710-page volume presents the birdlife of the western half of Pennsylvania in a degree of completeness and exactness that only Mr. Todd was capable of doing. Nothing of importance is overlooked or escapes the critical evaluation of the author. Thus it is *the* standard against which all future studies of western Penn-

Winter bird watching in the Pocono Mountains, Pennsylvania.

sylvania's birdlife must be compared and evaluated. Adding to the charm and value of the book are the many fine color plates painted by noted bird artist and ornithologist George Miksch Sutton.

A New Jersey Study

The rich birdlife of coastal New Jersey, especially at Cape May Point and nearby areas, has received the attention of generations of ornithologists and birdwatchers extending back to the days of John James Audubon and Alexander Wilson. However, nobody conducted a more careful or accurate accounting of Cape May's birds, or presented the information with more skill and love, than Witmer Stone in his classic *Bird Studies at Old Cape May*, published in two splendid volumes by the Delaware Valley Ornithological Club of Philadelphia. As one reads Stone's delightful historical and species accounts, one receives much more than the facts and figures of the birdlife of Cape May as it changed over long periods of time. Indeed, one receives a feeling of the area and tastes its flavor, because of the grace and charm in which the information is presented. As an added bonus the books are illustrated with the splendid drawings of Earl L. Poole, Conrad Roland, and others plus maps and photographs by some of the leading birdwatchers of the day. *Bird Studies at Old Cape May* is a book of value far beyond the circle of bird enthusiasts. It is a work of literature and deserves to be read frequently by all birdwatchers and birdlovers of the historic Cape May area.

Some New York Studies

Of all the locality bird studies published in North America, the one that impresses me as *the* finest and most exhaustive was done for the New York City region by John Bull and is titled *Birds of the New York Area*.

Building on a long and rich foundation of earlier bird studies in the area, by generations of skilled ornithologists and birdwatchers, Bull gathered and evaluated every scrap of available information to achieve a degree of comprehensiveness not included in any other regional bird book. Sight records, preserved specimens in museums and other collections, published records, and new information all were collected then critically examined to produce this monumental book. The result is that the birdlife of the New York City region now is known better, and in more detail, than that of any other comparable area in North America. Thus *Birds of the New York Area* easily can be used as *the* model study for locality birdwatchers. Particular attention should be given to Bull's critical and demanding standards—and his willingness to reject those sight or other records not grounded firmly upon solid fact.

In addition to the critical standards used to accept records for this book, the format of the work also is ideal and provides an excellent summary of the status of each species for the region.

If the birdlife of the New York City region is interesting, no less interesting is the birdlife of famous and beautiful Adirondack Park in upstate New York. Spread over some six million acres of public and private lands, Adirondack Park is one of the largest parks of its kind anywhere in the United States. As one would

Cape May Point, New Jersey—one of North America's famous bird-watching locations.

expect, it is the home of a rich assortment of birds. More than 150 species nest in the park, and over 250 species have been seen there over the years. Of particular interest are species such as three-toed woodpeckers, Spruce Grouse, Common Ravens, Gray-cheeked Thrushes, and others. To compile and summarize the wealth of ornithological and bird-watching information documented for the Adirondacks over the years and prepare that information for book form was a huge task—but one done with skill and excellence by Bruce McP. Beehler in his excellent *Birdlife of the Adirondack Park*, published by the Adirondack Mountain Club. Like so many other regional works already discussed in this chapter, this Airondack Park book also provides a firm foundation upon which future regional studies of Airondack birdlife can be established.

The six million acres of Adirondack Park, in upstate New York, is prime bird-watching country. Photo by New York State Department of Environmental Conservation.

An Ohio Study

Some 30 miles east of Columbus, Ohio, one finds famous Buckeye Lake whose birdlife was studied in detail and made famous by Milton B. Trautman in his classic *The Birds of Buckeye Lake, Ohio*. As a result of this model field study, at least 282 species of birds are documented solidly for the Buckeye Lake area in a manner that provides a solid base against which future changes in the area's avifauna can be measured. Not only were sight observations collected and evaluated, but data on bird specimens from the area also add more substance to Trautman's work. The published result is essential not only to scientists working in the area, but also to recreational birdwatchers exploring the Buckeye Lake region.

A Georgia Study

Among ornithologists the name of Herbert L. Stoddard, Sr. is well known and highly respected. Best known for his classic book on the Bobwhite, it is hardly surprising that he also studied the general birdlife on his beloved Grady County, Georgia, and prepared a fine report on his results—*Birds of Grady County, Georgia*, published after his death.

The center of Stoddard's efforts was on his splendid Sherwood Plantation, and from there he explored other nearby plantations and bird-rich areas with the aid of a devoted circle of friends. Specimens of some birds, sometimes found dead but at other times collected, were prepared as study skins and preserved as voucher specimens at the Tall Timbers Research Station in Florida. Critical evaluation of all specimens and sight records assured that Stoddard's report was accurate and a solid record of Grady County's past birdlife. Birdwatchers and ornithologists alike can thank Stoddard for his fine efforts.

A Florida Study

Brevard County, on Florida's east coast, is known widely as one of the best bird-watching locations in the eastern United States. Home of the Indian River Audubon Society, its birdlife has been studied for decades. In 1950, however, Allan and Helen Cruickshank—two of America's finest birdwatchers and bird photographers—began intensive field studies of the area's birdlife and in the years following a large and extremely accurate record of Brevard County's avifauna was developed. The results of those important field efforts now are published in *The Birds of Brevard County, Florida* by Allan D. and Helen G. Cruickshank. It is a splendid volume which all birdwatchers visiting eastern Florida will find of exceptional value in allowing them to evaluate their own observations. It also is a lasting memorial to one of America's great conservationists, as all who knew Allan Cruickshank will agree.

A Minnesota-Wisconsin Study

The St. Croix River Valley is an area containing about 11,550 square kilometers in the east-central portion of Minnesota and the northwestern section of Wisconsin. In many respects it acts as a biological crossroads for a wide variety of birdlife, and the valley's varied habitats provide excellent places for a bird fauna to live. Here birds from the south, north, east, and west tend to converge. Because of the uniqueness of the place, the present designation of the St. Croix as a National Scenic River, and the lack of good survey data on the region's birdlife, Craig A. Faaness conducted a careful study of the birds of the St. Croix River Valley from 1966 to 1980 and documented the past and present occurrence of 314 species of birds. This information, of interest not only to birdwatchers and ornithologists but also land use managers and land use specialists, was published by the United States Fish and Wildlife Service in a report entitled *Birds of the St. Croix River Valley: Minnesota and Wisconsin*. The book is particularly useful because it contains details on the status, migration, nesting, and habitat for each species. As in all such reports, there also is a detailed bibliography containing other pertinent publications on the birds of the area. Like so many reports of this type, therefore, it serves as a basic foundation upon which future birdwatchers and ornithologists can build future lists of the area's birdlife.

A Texas Study

During the early years of this century, the birdlife of Brewster County, Texas, in which Big Bend National Park now is located, was poorly known. By 1937, however, enough information on the birdlife of this section of southwestern Texas was available to allow Josselyn Van Tyne and George Miksch Sutton to publish *The Birds of Brewster County, Texas*. It reported on the status of 215 species of birds based upon 425 man-days of field study by these authors, as well as additional information obtained by a few earlier ornithologists. The Van Tyne and Sutton report was important because it provided some of the basic field data needed to justify the creation in 1944 of Big Bend National Park.

Today, thanks to the efforts of additional birdwatchers, the birds of this splendid and important park are known more perfectly still. Indeed, at least 385 species of birds now are reported on the park's checklist according to Roland H. Wauer in *Birds of Big Bend National Park and Vicinity*.

Not every area one studies, of course, will be designated as a national park. Nevertheless, the fact that detailed bird records were available in published form was a great asset to those persons working for the creation of Big Bend National Park. Clearly accurate records of the birdlife of a county sometimes can have value in addition to their worth to birdwatchers and ornithologists. Not infrequently that added worth takes the form of tools useful to conservationists involved in efforts to preserve and protect unique wildlife or other ecological areas.

An Oregon Study

Birdwatchers and ornithologists have not neglected the western United States as an area in which to conduct locality bird studies, even though many more such studies probably have been made in the East. Jackson County, Oregon, is one case in point. Located in southwestern Oregon, it borders California on the south and is about 113 kilometers from the Pacific Ocean.

Four major plant communities exist in Jackson County and thus influence the distribution of birds in the area: Chaparral-Oak Community, Mixed Conifer Forest, True Fir Forest, and Timberline

Part of Big Bend National Park, Texas. Photo by U.S. National Park Service.

Forest. In addition, two major mountain ranges are located in the county, the Cascade and Siskiyou Mountain systems.

Against this background, M. Ralph Browning conducted a detailed and important locality bird study in Jackson County and surrounding areas using not only his own field data but also information gathered over the years by other birdwatchers, plus published records, specimens, and related sources of information. The final result, documenting the occurrence of 259 species in the county, is presented as *The Distribution and Occurrence of the Birds of Jackson County, Oregon, and Surrounding Areas* and published by Browning in the *North American Fauna* series issued by the United States Fish and Wildlife Service. A particularly important feature of this report is the use of quantitative abundance scales to establish the relative abundance of each species. In addition, specific criteria are used to rate the frequency and seasonal occurrence of each species. Future birdwatchers will therefore have very exact and specific information upon which new information can be compared.

For the most part, the rating scales used are the nonbreeding abundance scales developed by Robert Arbib and published in 1957 in *American Birds* (11: 63–64). Only minor modifications were made on the original Arbib standards.

Restricted Locality Studies

While many locality studies deal with the birds of a particular county, there are a good many restricted locality studies that focus on the birds of smaller geographic areas. Documenting the birdlife of a particular state game land or wildlife management area is especially worthwhile with nearly unlimited opportunities available to interested birdwatchers. Many state wildlife agencies own and operate such wildlife areas, yet few of these public lands have their birdlife documented in published reports or even rough field notes. Birdwatchers are ideally equipped to resolve this situation and take over the task of studying and documenting the birdlife of such state lands. In Pennsylvania, for example, there are several hundred state game lands whose combined size numbers well over one million acres. Few, if any, bird studies have ever been conducted on most of these lands although there are a few exceptions. It is time, therefore, that such field studies were made so that accurate and comprehensive inventories of the birdlife of these areas are available for proper use of such property for the benefit of all wildlife resources rather than just game species.

One state game land that I have studied during autumn for more than a quarter century is Bake Oven Knob and its vicinity in northern Lehigh County, Pennsylvania. This is an extremely well-known autumn hawk lookout. Hawk watchers and birdwatchers generally visit it every autumn from far and near. More than 7,900 hours have been spent documenting the birdlife of the Knob. The result is a list of 162 species of birds sighted during autumn. Information of this type makes Bake Oven Knob one of the best known state game lands in Pennsylvania as far as its birdlife is concerned.

In addition to state wildlife areas, state and other parks also provide excellent opportunities for similar field studies. Indeed,

Bake Oven Knob, center background, is a state game land in eastern Pennsylvania and the site of intensive, long term bird migration studies.

all over this nation, there are such public lands that need detailed inventories of their birdlife. Why not select one and begin a restricted locality bird study for a few years? Eventual publication of the results can add to ornithological knowledge of an area as well as provide needed wildlife information useful to planners and others in the preparation of regional development, environmental impact, and other documents.

BREEDING BIRD ATLASES

One of the more important recent trends in locality bird watching is the preparation of a breeding bird atlas for a particular geographic area such as a county or state. An atlas contains maps of the locations of known, suspected, or implied nesting of species known to occur within the state or area being considered, or a map showing the general breeding range of the species in question. In the eastern United States, most bird atlases cover an entire state for a period of five years. Within the state, a grid of blocks measuring 5×5 kilometers (25^2 kilometers) is established and each of these grid blocks is carefully studied. On the other hand, in the western United States variations on atlases cover a so-called Latilong, which is an area consisting of one degree of latitude by one degree of longitude without any specified time period being established. In Canada, a third type of grid block system is used measuring at least 10 kilometers on a side or 100^2 kilometers.

In 1981, a Northeastern Breeding Bird Atlas Conference attempted to develop a uniform methodology for all North American breeding bird atlas projects, but the failure of the organizers of the conference to open the gathering to all interested persons (and thus obtain as wide a variety of opinions and comments as possible) rather than inviting only selected persons seriously limited the value of the effort. Nevertheless, some worthwhile results were achieved including the development of a list of criteria for determining the breeding status of birds. Persons interested in working on breeding bird atlases are not required to follow these suggestions, but can use them as worthwhile guidelines.

In the United States and Canada, breeding bird surveys which produce the information used in the preparation of breeding bird atlases usually are conducted by amateur and professional ornithologists and birdwatchers, thus giving everybody plenty of opportunities to participate and contribute to the overall effort.

The first breeding bird atlases were prepared in Great Britain, but the projects now are spreading rapidly in one form or another in North America and elsewhere around the world. The North American Ornithological Atlas Committee (NAOAC) coordinates the work here and can be contacted through Dr. Miklos D. F. Udvardy at the Department of Biological Sciences, California State University, Sacramento, California 95819.

In one form or another, several states and provinces including California (Marin County), Colorado, Connecticut, Maine, Maryland, Massachusetts, Montana, Nebraska, New Hampshire, New Jersey, New York, Ontario, Rhode Island, Utah, Vermont, and Wyoming have completed breeding bird atlases or currently have them in preparation. In addition, British Columbia, Delaware, Florida, the Canadian Maritime Provinces, and Michigan are planning such atlases.

Most breeding bird atlases deal with all species of birds nesting in the area being studied, but it also is possible to deal only with selected types of birds and to prepare an atlas of their breeding or geographic distribution. Within recent years the United States Fish and Wildlife Service has produced some excellent examples of this special or restricted type of atlas dealing especially with seabirds and colonial waterbirds. An example is the *Catalog of Alaskan Seabird Colonies*. It plots on large maps the locations of all seabird colonies known to exist in Alaska and the species of birds that occupy the colonies. Thus it is an important tool for seabird conservationists because it documents the locations of these sensitive wildlife areas. Similar atlases of nesting coastal waterbird colonies also are available for the area from Maine to Florida, the Gulf of Mexico, and California. Others also are in preparation. In time, breeding raptor atlases also might be prepared for certain selected areas, as well as for other selected bird species. Birdwatchers can participate in these projects by sending information to project directors.

BIRD OBSERVATORIES

The concept and establishment of bird observatories began in Europe about a century ago, now is operating in North America as well, and is an important part of the overall scientific effort to gather new information about some aspects of the lives of birds, especially their migrations. A bird observatory, therefore, is a research station, usually with a building containing laboratories, a research library, limited living quarters, and other areas all located on a parcel of land along a coast, mountain, or other geographic feature which birds use regularly at seasonal intervals and in large numbers.

Much of the work of a bird observatory involves the banding of birds. For this work one needs a good deal of training and experience, as well as special permits from the state and federal governments. However, some bird observatory work also involves observation of birds engaged in a variety of activities and birdwatchers certainly can help to aid such efforts. Too, there always is a large amount of record keeping involved, as well as analysis of data collected by the bird banders. Therefore the talents of many people are welcome if one has a serious interest in avian research.

At the present time there are only about a dozen bird observatories operating in North America. Two of the most active are the Manomet Bird Observatory in Massachusetts and the Point

Reyes Bird Observatory in California. A good many other ongoing ornithological research projects in many sections of North America, while not named bird observatories, nevertheless essentially carry out the same type of work. My own migration studies at Bake Oven Knob in eastern Pennsylvania provide a case in point, as do the bird-banding studies at Powdermill Nature Reserve in western Pennsylvania, the latter being sponsored by the Carnegie Museum of Natural History.

REGIONAL PHOTOGRAPHIC FILES

Many years ago ornithologists accepted records of the presence of birds in an area only when supported by one or more specimens collected in an area and later preserved and deposited in a museum collection. Such specimens provided ornithologists with the oppurtunity to examine and verify the validity of records.

Today collecting birds is prohibited by law, except for rigidly controlled educational and scientific purposes. As a result, most current records of the presence of unusually rare or otherwise interesting birds in an area are based on sight observations of birdwatchers and/or photographs taken of the birds in question. In the case of the latter, copies of color slides or other types of photographs should be deposited in a regional photographic file perhaps maintained at a local museum or other suitable institution. Such photographs always should contain the name of the photographer, the exact location where the bird was photographed, the exact and full date when the photo was taken, and any additional related information of importance. Photographs can provide vital scientific documentation for unusual bird records for a particular area and also serve the same function as specimens did in the past—namely allowing future ornithologists the opportunity to recheck the validity of past records.

A regional photographic file also can serve as a depository for photographs of nests and eggs of birds found in a particular area, thus providing clear documentation that certain species nest in an area. As with photos of rare birds, each photograph of a nest and eggs should have marked on it the identity of the species, the date and exact location of the nest, the name of the photographer, and any other significant information relating to the record. This type of information rarely is available for most areas and can be of very considerable scientific importance to future ornithologists wishing to look at past breeding bird records in the light of new information. Thus the establishment of regional photographic files provides local or regional birdwatchers with an excellent and lasting project in which they can participate.

PROJECT VIREO

An alternative and more comprehensive version of the regional photographic file concept is the establishment of a national or international file of bird documentation photographs for use by scientists, artists, and educators. Such a project and file is being established at the Academy of Natural Sciences of Philadelphia where the photographs are stored in a central collection and coded to computers for quick access. The project, named VIREO (Vis-

Nest and eggs of a Spotted Sandpiper. Photographs such as this, with basic location and date information marked on the back, provide important nesting documentation.

ual Resources for Ornithology), is unique because the Academy also has available its major collection of more than 160,000 bird study skins for comparative purposes with photographs.

Any color or black and white photographs that document bird biology, behavior, or distribution are of interest to scientists for inclusion in the collection. In addition, historic photographs of ornithologists or matters dealing with ornithology also are wanted. Photographs that meet portrait quality of birds, ornithologists, or ornithological activities or techniques are desirable. Since the collection is worldwide in scope, there are no restrictions on the species of birds shown in photographs. Photographs of bird habitats also are requested, and in some instances even photographs of art objects dealing with birds might be accepted for inclusion in the VIREO collection.

Worthwhile as such a collection is, now and in the future, certain legal and other aspects should always be resolved in a proper manner before photographs are sent to any collections. Among the most important are ownership of photographs, ownership of reproduction rights to such photographs, ownership of copyrights, and amounts and methods of payment of any royalties for use or sale of such materials. The Academy of Natural Sciences provides a variety of contractual arrangements for photographs, but one always should be prepared to insist upon different terms of a contract if the terms being offered are not satisfactory— and reject participation in a project if terms can't be agreed upon to the photographer's complete satisfaction.

Full details on VIREO can be obtained by writing: Director VIREO, Academy of Natural Sciences, 19th and The Parkway, Philadelphia, Pennsylvania 19103.

PRESERVATION OF BIRD RECORDS

As a final comment on this chapter, it is necessary here to discuss the final preservation of notebooks and other written bird records from a particular area. All too often dedicated birdwatchers who keep detailed notebooks of their observations, sometimes for decades, fail to take any, or adequate provisions to assure the proper archival disposition of such records with the result that a lifetime of dedicated work may be discarded or otherwise lost to ornithology. Helen Cruickshank, for example, in *The Birds of Brevard County, Florida*, writes of "a distinguished ornithologist who for many years kept the most meticulous records of the birds in his area. At his death, the records were all destroyed."

The example of which Mrs. Cruickshank spoke is far from the only sad example of important ornithological records being lost to future generations. There are many other examples as well. Not infrequently, such records not only covered decades but also provided vital comparative information gathered prior to the impact of pesticides, habitat destruction, and development upon birdlife in many areas. Information of this type, therefore, is vital to determining long-term population changes in the birdlife of an area and is of great historic importance.

Fortunately there is no reason why important bird records need be lost as estates are settled. All one need do, *without delay*, is include a provision in one's will indicating clearly where such bird record notebooks and other records shall be deposited. Some suitable examples are local historical society libraries, state museums, natural history museums, nature centers, or college or university libraries. Particular care, however, should be taken to be certain that the institution selected is capable of giving such historic records proper care and protection—including protection against improper use by unqualified persons—and that such institutions fully recognize the value and importance of such records.

There are several ornithological archives in the United States that might be suitable depositories including the library at the Academy of Natural Sciences of Philadelphia (19th and The Parkway, Philadelphia, Pennsylvania 19103) and the library of Cornell University at Ithaca, New York. However, if these collections are located any significant distance from the geographic location where the records were made, local people needing access to the information may not be able to visit these institutions or otherwise arrange to use the records. Therefore, geographic location of a depository also is an important factor in determining where one should arrange to deposit his or her record notebooks as an estate is settled.

ADDITIONAL READING

Bagg, A. C. and S. A. Eliot, Jr.
  1937 *Birds of the Connecticut Valley in Massachusetts.* Hampshire Bookshop, Hampshire, Massachusetts
Beck, H. H.
  1924 *A Chapter on the Ornithology of Lancaster County, Pennsylvania.* Lewis Historical Publishing Co., Inc., New York, N. Y.
Beehler, B. McP.
  1978 *Birdlife of the Adirondack Park.* Adirondack Mountain Club, Glens Falls, N.Y.
Browning, M.R.
  1975 The Distribution and Occurrence of the Birds of Jackson County, Oregon, and Surrounding Areas. *North American Fauna* No. 70: 1–69.
Bull, J.
  1964 *Birds of the New York Area.* Harper & Row, Publishers, New York, N. Y.
Clapp, R. B., R. C. Banks, D. Morgan-Jacobs, and W. A. Hoffman
  1982 *Marine Birds of the Southeastern United States and Gulf of Mexico.* Part I. U. S. Fish and Wildlife Service, Washington, D. C.
Cruickshank, A. D. and H. G. Cruickshank
  1980 *The Birds of Brevard County, Florida.* Florida Press, Inc., Orlando, Fla.
Durman, R. (Ed.)
  1976 *Bird Observatories in Britain and Ireland.* T. & A. D. Poyser Ltd., Berkhamsted, England.
Erwin, R. M. and C. E. Korschgen
  1979 *Coastal Waterbird Colonies: Maine to Virginia, 1977.* U. S. Fish and Wildlife Service, Washington, D. C.
Faanes, C. A.
  1981 Birds of the St. Croix River Valley: Minnesota and Wisconsin. *North American Fauna* No. 73: 1–196.
Forsell, D. J. and P. J. Gould
  1981 *Distribution and Abundance of Marine Birds and Mammals Wintering in the Kodiak Area of Alaska.* U. S. Fish and Wildlife Service, Washington, D. C.
Frey, E. S.
  1943 *The Centennial Check-List of the Birds of Cumberland County, Pennsylvania and Her Borders.* Published by the author, Lemoyne, Pa.
Fritts, T. H., and R. F. Reynolds
  1981 *Pilot Study of the Marine Mammals, Birds and Turtles in OCS Areas of the Gulf of Mexico.* U. S. Fish and Wildlife Service, Washington, D. C.

Hebard, F. V.
   1959 *Water Birds of Penobscot Bay.* Portland Society of Natural History, Portland, Maine.
   1960 *The Land Birds of Penobscot Bay.* Portland Society of Natural History, Portland, Maine.

Laughlin, S. B., D. P. Kibble, and P. F. J. Eagles
   1982 Atlasing the Distribution of the Breeding Birds of North America. *American Birds,* 36 (1): 6–19.

Osborn, R. G. and T. W. Custer
   1978 *Herons and Their Allies: Atlas of Atlantic Coast Colonies, 1975 and 1976.* U. S. Fish and Wildlife Service, Washington, D. C.

Poole, E. L.
   1947 *A Half Century of Bird Life in Berks County, Pennsylvania.* Bulletin 19. Reading Public Museum and Art Gallery, Reading, Pa.

Portnoy, J. W., R. M. Erwin, and T. W. Custer
   1981 *Atlas of Gull and Tern Colonies: North Carolina to Key West, Florida (including Pelicans, Cormorants and Skimmers).* U. S. Fish and Wildlife Service, Washington, D. C.

Sowls, A. L., A. R. DeGange, J. W. Nelson, and G. S. Lester
   1980 *Catalog of California Seabird Colonies.* U. S. Fish and Wildlife Service, Washington, D. C.

Sowls, A. L., S. A. Hatch, and C. J. Lensink
   1978 *Catalog of Alaskan Seabird Colonies.* U. S. Fish and Wildlife Service, Washington, D. C.

Stoddard, H. L., Sr.
   1978 Birds of Grady County, Georgia. No. 21. *Bulletin Tall Timbers Research Station,* Tallahassee, Fla.

Stone, W.
   1937 *Bird Studies at Old Cape May.* Two volumes. Delaware Valley Ornithological Club, Philadelphia, Pa.

Street, P. B.
   1954 Birds of the Pocono Mountains, Pennsylvania. *Cassinia,* 41: 3–76.
   1975 Birds of the Pocono Mountains, 1955–1975. *Cassinia,* 55: 3–16.

Todd, W. E. C.
   1940 *Birds of Western Pennsylvania.* University of Pittsburgh Press, Pittsburgh, Pa.

Trautman, M. E.
   1940 The Birds of Buckeye Lake, Ohio. *Misc. Publications Museum of Zoology University of Michigan,* 44: 1–466.

Van Tyne, J. and G. M. Sutton
   1937 The Birds of Brewster County, Texas. *Misc. Publications Museum of Zoology University of Michigan,* 37: 1–119.

Vardaman, J. M.
  1980   *Call Collect, Ask for Birdman.* St. Martin's Press, New York, N. Y.
Wauer, R. H.
  1973   *Birds of Big Bend National Park and Vicinity.* University of Texas Press, Austin, Texas
Wheat, M. C., Jr.
  1981   Compiling the Breeding Bird Atlas. *Bird Watcher's Digest*, 3 (4): 24–29.

Chapter 5

Projects With Waterfowl

The rich waterfowl resources of North America provide bird-watchers with exceptional opportunities to engage in special study projects. Not only are many species common or abundant, but most are large birds, easily observed, and relatively easy to identify and count. Thus swans, geese, and ducks are ideal subjects for birders to get to know better. There are many ways to do this. The projects described here are only a few that are particularly exciting and enjoyable opportunities.

WHISTLING SWANS

For a number of years ornithologists under the direction of William Sladen at Johns Hopkins University have engaged in a long-range study of the migrations and other movements of Whistling Swans in an effort to define with accuracy the major flyways used by these birds in spring and autumn and to learn more about their overall ecology and biology on both the breeding and wintering grounds. This is accomplished by trapping the birds alive and unharmed on their wintering grounds, the Arctic nesting grounds, or occasionally elsewhere, then putting a numbered plastic neck collar on each bird along with numbered leg bands issued by the United States Fish and Wildlife Service. The neck collars are color coded to indicate the general geographic areas where the birds were captured. In North America, for example, black collars identify birds captured on their wintering grounds in the Southeast or Chesapeake Bay; yellow identifies swans captured between the breeding and wintering grounds; red is used for birds captured in Arctic Canada; blue for Alaska; and green for the Pacific Coast states. Because each collar has a number, large enough to be read by skilled observers from a distance using a telescope, opportunities to engage in fascinating swan projects are present. One can, for example, make repeated visits to areas where Whistling Swans gather during migration, or just prior to it, and try to read the numbers on the collars worn by some swans. A detailed record of collar color, number, location, and date then can be sent to Dr. Sladen at Johns Hopkins University thereby filling in some of the gaps in our knowledge of the movements of the species generally and of individual birds. Indeed, one can even go further and "adopt" a swan by paying a specified fee to "sponsor" a bird and thus help to provide financial support for the research.

Theodore R. Hake, an experienced birdwatcher and former Audubon wildlife warden from York, Pennsylvania, is one such person who has devoted countless hours over a period of years to this effort. He uses a large astronomical telescope to locate the swans wearing neck collars along the lower Susquehanna River in eastern Pennsylvania. His results have been impressive. He has contributed substantial quantities of vital data to the project. The birds not only are examined carefully on the river, early in the morning, in late autumn and early spring, but additional searches are made of nearby fields on which the birds sometimes gather in large numbers to eat leftover corn resulting from the use of mechanical corn pickers. These daily gatherings also attract birdwatchers from far and near and are yearly becoming increasingly popular birding attractions even to people who prefer not to engage in research. More than one farmer, on whose land the birds rest and feed, also expressed keen interest in the birds and a delight in having the wild creatures on their property.

Unfortunately, some farmers object to the presence of the birds on their land, and occasionally a few swans are shot illegally. Birdwatchers, therefore, have excellent opportunities to speak on behalf of the big birds in order to develop goodwill for them when farmers and some sportsmen object to their presence. Food habits, migration routes, and recreational values (including money brought into communities by birdwatchers looking at the swans) can be discussed in such educational efforts.

Persons wishing more information on participation in the swan project can write to Swan Research Program, Chesapeake Bay Foundation, Inc., P. O. Box 1709, Annapolis, Maryland 21404. Qualified observers always are needed to assist in the project.

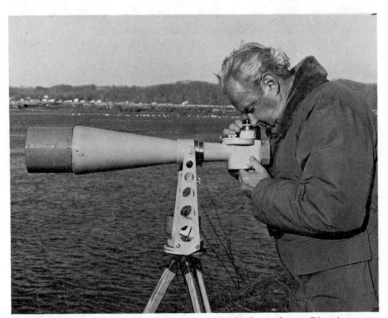

Theodore R. Hake observing Whistling Swans on the Susquehanna River in eastern Pennsylvania.

Migrating Whistling Swans along the Susquehanna River in eastern Pennsylvania.

BLACK BRANT SURVEY

Every year, from March to early May, birdwatchers and naturalists associated with the Mitlenatch Field Naturalist Society in British Columbia count the numbers of Brant migrating past the east coast of Vancouver Island. Keen observers and qualified birdwatchers in the area are welcome to assist in the program. For more details and instructions for assisting, contact Mrs. J. Conway, 2147 S. Island Highway, Campbell River, British Columbia, Canada V92 2S9.

GOOSE FLOCK SIZES

It is a rare citizen, and even rarer birdwatcher, who has not watched, listened to, and thrilled at the seasonal migrations of Canada Geese, or other species of geese, each spring and autumn. Again and again, as part of the changing seasons, we all enjoy these bird migrations. Some years ago I was astonished to discover, however, that little was known about the size of flocks of migrating Canada Geese. As I searched for information on the subject, I discovered that very few people had ever bothered to count the numbers of birds contained in the wedges of birds winging across our skies! As a result, several associates and I decided to try to count the numbers of Canada Geese contained in as many flocks of migrating birds in autumn as possible to throw some light onto the fascinating subject. The location from which this study was done was the summit of Bake Oven Knob, an important hawk migration lookout in eastern Pennsylvania, past which thousands of migrating Canada Geese fly every autumn. The study began in 1962 and continued through 1975. During that period we counted 759 flocks of geese containing 43,595 birds. There was an average of 57.4 birds per flock.

It would be worthwhile if other birdwatchers conducted similar projects elsewhere where large numbers of Canada Geese, or

A flock of migrating Canada Geese.

other species of geese, appear during migration. It is a simple project which anyone with binoculars or a telescope can enjoy. For best results, goose counting efforts should be conducted for a period of several years with thousands of birds included in the sample. Then the results can be summarized for publication in one of the many ornithological journals issued in North America.

DIVING DUCKS

While it is interesting to determine the sizes of flocks of migrating geese, it is just as interesting and fascinating to measure (time) the duration of the dives made by the various species of diving ducks native to North America. Again, relatively little information of this type is available. With the aid of a stopwatch, one can easily time the durations of the dives of scaup, goldeneyes, mergansers, and other diving ducks, then tabulate the information, and publish it in a journal.

WATERFOWL SURVEYS

The composition and size of waterfowl populations change frequently due to seasonal and other factors. Thus it is enjoyable to make surveys of the species, and numbers of each species, of waterfowl one sees on local lakes, ponds, or rivers. Such surveys, if conducted at frequent intervals during all or portions of the year (such as autumn through spring), can eventually reveal patterns of change in the composition of waterfowl populations in a given geographic area.

In New York State, for example, just such winter waterfowl surveys are conducted by birdwatchers cooperating with the Federation of New York State Bird Clubs. The state is divided into ten regions and the results of the counts are presented for each region, which allows the entire state or any of the ten regions to be compared. In 1981, for example, all species of waterfowl showed reductions in numbers reported except Brant, scaup, Buffleheads, and Common Mergansers. On a more long-term trend, the Canada Goose, American Black Duck, American Wigeon, Redhead, Canvasback, scaup (both species), goldeneye (both species), scoters (three species), and Red-breasted Merganser each showed declines in populations compared with the average for the period 1973–1980. On the other hand, some species showed population increases compared with the 1973–1980 period, including the Brant, Mallard, Gadwall, Bufflehead, Oldsquaw, and Common Merganser. Generally the counts are made sometime during January, and the information is published in *The Kingbird* as an annual report. Birdwatchers all over the state, therefore, soon learn of the trends in waterfowl populations. To facilitate record keeping during the survey, and in reporting the results to the project coordinators, a special data form is used, a sample of which is printed here. Similar data forms also could be used by birdwatchers in other states when they begin such waterfowl surveys.

The waterfowl studies of Dale Rex Coman along the Delaware River bordering New Jersey and Pennsylvania provide another example of waterfowl surveys. This project was carried out between September 1943 and August 1944 in the general Camden

The Mallard is a species often seen on waterfowl surveys.

NEW YORK STATE WATERFOWL COUNT, JANUARY 19___   REGION___   PAGE__OF__

PARTY LEADER	DATE	# OF HRS	AREA COVERED
A			
B			
C			
D			
E			
F			
G			
H			
J			
K			

	A	B	C	D	E	F	G	H	J	K	TOTAL
LOON, COMMON											
RED-THROATED											
GREBE, RED-NECKED											
HORNED											
PIED-BILLED											
CORMORANT, GREAT											
DBL-CRESTED											
SWAN, MUTE											
WHISTLING											
GOOSE, CANADA											
BRANT											
SNOW											
MALLARD											
BLACK DUCK											
MALLARD X BLACK											
GADWALL											
PINTAIL											
TEAL, GR-WINGED											
BLUE-WINGED											
WIGEON, AMERICAN											
EUROPEAN											
NORTHERN SHOVELER											
WOOD DUCK											
REDHEAD											
RING-NECKED DUCK											
CANVASBACK											
SCAUP - ALL											
GREATER											
LESSER											
GOLDENEYE, COMMON											
BARROW'S											
BUFFLEHEAD											
OLDSQUAW											
EIDER, COMMON											
KING											
SCOTER, WH-WINGED											
SURF											
BLACK											
RUDDY DUCK											
MERGANSER, HOODED											
COMMON											
RED-BREASTED											
AMERICAN COOT											
TOTALS											

The data form used by the Federation of New York State Bird Clubs, Inc., in their annual waterfowl surveys. Courtesy of Federation of New York State Bird Clubs, Inc.

area, along about 40 miles of the New Jersey side of the river, and makes a fascinating comparison with similar information collected by Julian Potter in 1918 in the same general area. The one obvious result is that the waterfowl population noted in 1918 was much less numerous than in the 1943–44 survey. While a variety of ecological and hunting factors might be responsible, in part, for the drastic changes in numbers of birds seen, it is nevertheless likely that waterfowl populations have increased in the area. In addition to the historic aspect of the work, the project also showed a clear seasonal difference in the numbers of waterfowl in the area. Mid-November was, by far, the period when the largest numbers of waterfowl were present, whereas spring counts were tiny in comparison. Apparently waterfowl using the area in autumn migration follow different migration routes during spring. Thus historic and species composition aspects of waterfowl along this section of the Delaware River were documented. Perhaps birdwatchers sometime in the future will conduct new waterfowl surveys in the same area and again compare the results with the information now available for 1918 and 1943–44. It is these types of repeated comparisons over long periods of time that give scientists and birdwatchers important insights into changes in populations of wild birds.

WOOD DUCK NEST BOX PROJECTS

Anyone who has ever seen a male Wood Duck in full breeding plumage will be quick to agree that these most colorful of North American waterfowl are splendid birds. At the same time this species readily accepts nest boxes as nest sites. Thus birdwatchers and other waterfowl conservationists have an excellent opportunity to aid local Wood Duck populations by establishing nest boxes near lakes, ponds, and streams with adequate protective cover nearby to allow ducklings reasonable chances for survival until they are able to fly. Assistance in proper nest box site evaluation and selection often is available from state and federal wildlife agencies.

While the desire to help Wood Ducks is commendable, it can't be stressed too strongly that *box construction must be done correctly* or not at all. Among the key considerations to keep in mind are the following.

1. Proper selection of box support is important. Trees can be

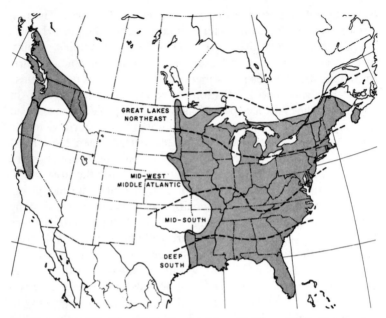

Breeding range of the Wood Duck. Reprinted from McGilvrey (1968). Map courtesy of U. S. Fish and Wildlife Service.

used, but generally it is perferable to put the boxes on wood or metal posts.

2. Use of a predator protection guard is always to be used. Such a guard is a metal shield fastened below the box and extending no less than 18 inches from the post support.

3. Nest boxes should be placed along the edge or over a body of water about 10 feet above the water or ground surface. The predator guard also should be at least 3 feet above the high water level.

4. A layer of sawdust or wood shavings, at least 3 inches deep, should be put inside the bottom of the box to give the female a safe spot on which she may lay her eggs.

5. Don't forget to repair and clean nest boxes every January. Nest material inside the box should be replaced at that time.

6. Some conservationists put two or more boxes on the same

supporting post to increase productivity. Unlike most birds, Wood Ducks tolerate such close nests.

A variety of more or less standard box designs are readily available from state and federal wildlife agencies for use on Wood Duck projects. The box illustrated here is one recommended by the United States Fish and Wildlife Service in its Wildlife Leaflet 510 "Nest Boxes for Wood Ducks" and can be constructed easily. After the box is constructed, it is important *not* to paint or otherwise treat the wood. Additional features on the box should include an oval-shaped entrance hole, with the broadest measurement horizontal, a piece of screen or hardware cloth tacked inside the box underneath the entrance hole to help the ducklings leave the box, inside treatment with Lysol or another disinfectant to discourage wasps and bees from using the box, and the use of rustproof screws and nails.

WATERFOWL REFUGES

Wetland preservation is vital to maintaining adequate waterfowl populations. Thus the Canadian and United States Fish and Wildlife Services, as well as Ducks Unlimited in North America, have spent millions of dollars to protect wetlands and set them aside as waterfowl breeding areas as described in *North American Ducks, Geese & Swans*. Persons wishing to aid such government efforts can do so readily by buying a so-called federal duck stamp at most post offices. Some states also sell state duck stamps as well. In addition, some birdwatchers might wish to join Ducks Unlimited (P. O. Box 66300, Chicago, Illinois 60666) to aid their waterfowl refuge program.

Other wetlands, however, not protected by such impressive programs, also are equally important to waterfowl either as breeding sites, resting areas during migration, or wintering sites. They, too, should be preserved and protected. Birdwatchers also can play a role in working to establish such wetlands as refuges whenever possible. Perhaps it is a farmer's marsh or pond that can be preserved, or a corporation's wetland, or possibly a town or city's lake, pond, or marsh. Regardless of the ownership of the property, such efforts to establish waterfowl refuges will benefit ducks,

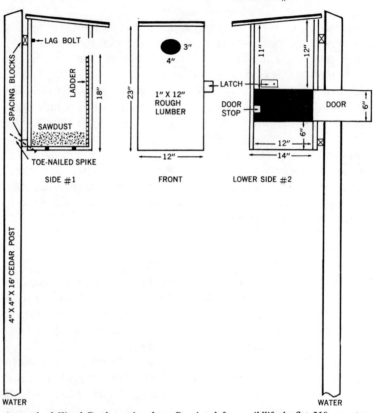

A standard Wood Duck nesting box. Reprinted from wildlife leaflet 510, courtesy U. S. Fish and Wildlife Service.

geese, and swans and also provide better bird-watching opportunities.

What, then, are some of the methods concerned persons can use to help to save wetlands that are so vital to the survival of waterfowl and various other aquatic birds? How can these methods be used to help wildlife?

Regardless if one is a private citizen or a member of a bird club, sportsman club, 4-H club, Boy or Girl Scout troop, senior citizens organization, or general service club, the methods useful

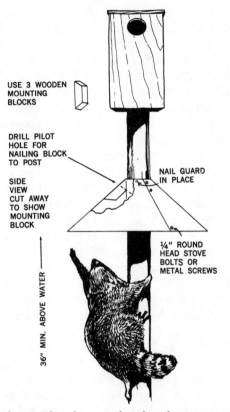

USE 3 WOODEN
MOUNTING
BLOCKS

DRILL PILOT
HOLE FOR
NAILING BLOCK
TO POST

NAIL GUARD
IN PLACE

SIDE
VIEW
CUT AWAY
TO SHOW
MOUNTING
BLOCK

¼" ROUND
HEAD STOVE
BOLTS OR
METAL SCREWS

36" MIN. ABOVE WATER

A cone-shaped, sheet-metal predator guard used on the support post below a Wood Duck nest box. Reprinted from wildlife leaflet 510, courtesy U. S. Fish and Wildlife Service.

in the battle to save wetlands can be much the same. For example, the first step in saving wetlands is to become aware of their existence in a given area. It is essential to conduct field surveys of all wetlands in a particular area, such as a county, in order to determine accurately which sites are important and which can be ignored. Use of topographic maps can be helpful in this effort. Wetlands generally are clearly marked on such maps which should make the location and inspection of the sites a relatively simple matter in many regions of the country.

After a site is inspected, and its possible value to waterfowl recognized, the next step is to conduct regular (perhaps weekly) surveys of the species and numbers of waterfowl that use the site. At least one year should be devoted to this aspect of the project and several years of information would be more valuable. A search of local birding and ornithological literature for pertinent published information also should be made. Information obtained in such published sources also should be included in one's evaluation of the wetland.

While these steps are in progress, somebody involved in the project also should determine if the the site is public property or owned privately. It is difficult to determine which situation is the more favorable, depending upon local attitudes of the people involved in ownership or control of the property. In either case, however, a short written report detailing the importance of the wetland to waterfowl (and other wildlife) and its ownership should be prepared and an adequate number of copies made to distribute to concerned persons in the community. Special care should be given to full and accurate documentation of the facts presented in the report, including proper credit for all published references cited.

At this point, there are various ways in which one might suggest that a wetland should be protected and preserved as a waterfowl refuge. In some cases, nothing more than a simple recommendation may be enough to have the area set aside as a refuge. In other instances, there may be objections from persons who wish to use the site for other purposes such as a supply of water for irrigation, boating, or landfill and development. If that is the case, professional help almost certainly will be needed to try to establish the refuge. Even then the project may fail. Nevertheless, there are sources of help available including asking for support and professional assistance from state and/or federal wildlife agencies, local bird study groups, and sympathetic politicians (especially if they are interested in waterfowl hunting or conservation).

If a property is owned privately, but available for purchase, professional assistance also should be obtained to accurately evaluate the value of the property. Perhaps a state wildlife agency's wetlands conservation funds, derived from the sale of state duck stamps, could be used to buy the property. In other cases the

United States Fish and Wildlife Service might become involved in purchases using funds derived from the sale of federal duck stamps. On the other hand, if the site is relatively small (but nevertheless locally important), it might be possible for a local bird club or Audubon Society to raise enough money to buy the property and establish a waterfowl refuge there. There are a few examples of this being done in the United States. Some state Audubon socieites also own and operate networks of wildlife sanctuaries, and it is possible that they would try to purchase or otherwise obtain such property to add to their already existing refuge network. In some instances involving very important sites, the National Audubon Society, Nature Conservancy, regional or local conservancies, Defenders of Wildlife, or other wildlife conservation organizations might become interested and try to obtain the site and maintain it as a waterfowl refuge. Each of these possible avenues should be explored carefully and thoroughly before they are eliminated.

Regardless of how a site is obtained, protected, and maintained as a waterfowl refuge, it is necessary to assure the continued protection of the wetland after it is secured. For example, local birdwatchers can form a committee to check the site regularly, around the year, to be certain no damage or unauthorized use (such as trash dumping) is done there. In addition, the refuge should be clearly marked as such with signs outlining ownership and use restrictions. Birdwatchers can help to maintain and replace these signs when necessary.

In some instances, a waterfowl refuge may become a very welcome and useful conservation-education facility for local bird clubs and nature study groups who can organize and operate special nature study trips to the refuge. Careful consideration must be given to which sections of the property should not be disturbed, however, so that wildlife will not suffer unnecessary disturbance. Nevertheless, many refuges serve as outstanding conservation-education facilities in the United States and Canada, and there seems little reason to expect that many (perhaps most) refuges can't be used for this purpose in at least some limited or restricted way, depending upon the nature of the site and the species of waterfowl and other wildlife that use it.

Public and private schools with environmental education pro-

grams also might welcome opportunities to use such newly established waterfowl refuges for a variety of field trip purposes.
Teachers and school administrators involved with biology and
other environmental studies should be contacted and thoroughly
informed of available opportunities at the refuge. It is ironic how
many school teachers responsible for teaching biology and environmental studies are not aware of important (sometimes even
major) wildlife refuges and attractions in close proximity to their
schools! In some cases, teachers may have to be given a mini-
course in the importance of the refuges, the wildlife that uses
them, and educational opportunities at such refuges, but this should
become a welcome opportunity to advance public interest in appreciation and understanding of wildlife. Birdwatchers can play
a useful role in this aspect of waterfowl refuge establishment and
use.

WATERFOWL IDENTIFICATION COURSE

Perhaps the most obvious way in which waterfowl can be used
as objects of study is to develop an informal, nontechnical waterfowl identification course designed to teach novice birdwatchers, hunters, and other people the basic skills needed to recognize
and identify common local waterfowl species. Swans, geese, and
ducks are ideally suited for this purpose because they are large,
often common, generally conspicuous in their wetland habitats,
and among the easier bird species to identify. Thus they provide
excellent subjects around which to design a beginner bird identification course and an excellent opportunity for experienced
birdwatchers to pass along some of their birding skills to newcomers.

Perhaps the first task in developing a waterfowl identification
course is to survey local lakes, ponds, marches, reservoirs, creeks,
streams, rivers, or other wetlands to determine which support the
largest variety and numbers of waterfowl species. The best spots
will usually serve nicely as the places to which field trips should
be taken to give course participants practical field experience. In
some sections of the United States, a national wildlife refuge may
be located nearby. Most federal refuges are excellent waterfowl
viewing areas, and certainly should be used for field trips if they
are nearby. Some refuges offer special educational programs pre-

sented by their staff if arranged in advance. Basic details about national wildlife refuges of particular importance to waterfowl, and directions for visiting them, are presented in my *North American Ducks, Geese & Swans*. Many state wildlife agencies also own and operate wildlife management areas, some of importance to waterfowl. They also may be suitable for visits by students of waterfowl identification.

The next step in developing a waterfowl identification course is to discuss the classification of waterfowl in an orderly manner, so that students will not only be able to recognize close evolutionary relationships between species, but also realize that segregation of related species into groups will aid in quick and accurate identification of the birds. In North America, for example, waterfowl generally can be separated into three very broad groups all contained in the family Anatidae—swans, geese, and ducks. On a more technical basis, various waterfowl authorities accept differing arrangements of waterfowl classification so that the placement of species in families, subfamilies, tribes, and related groups may differ from that printed in some field guides used by birdwatchers. Nevertheless, two widely used classifications are outlined here: that used by Roger Tory Peterson in *A Field Guide to the Birds* and in my own *North American Ducks, Geese & Swans,* shown as follows:

Family Anatidae: Swans, Geese, and Ducks
    Subfamily Cygninae: Swans
    Subfamily Anserinae: Geese
    Subfamily Dendrocygninae: Whistling Ducks
    Subfamily Anatinae: Surface-Feeding Ducks (Dabbling Ducks)
    Subfamily Aythyinae: Diving (Sea or Bay) Ducks
    Subfamily Oxyurinae: Ruddy and Masked (Stiff-tailed) Ducks
    Subfamily Merginae: Mergansers

In comparison, the classification used by Frank C. Bellrose in *Ducks, Geese & Swans of North America* and Paul A. Johnsgard in *Waterfowl of North America* is arranged as follows.

Family Anatidae: Swans, Geese, and Ducks
    Subfamily Anserinae: Whistling Ducks, Swans, and True Geese

Tribe Dendrocygnini: Whistling Ducks
Tribe Anserini: Swans and True Geese
Subfamily Anatinae: Ducks and Mergansers (North American)
Tribe Cairinini: Wood Duck
Tribe Anatini: Surface-Feeding (Dabbling or Marsh) Ducks
Tribe Aythyini: Diving (Sea or Bay) Ducks
Tribe Mergini: Eiders, Harlequin, Oldsquaw, Scoters,
Bufflehead, Goldeneyes, and Mergansers
Tribe Oxyurini: Ruddy and Masked (Stiff-tailed) Ducks

Regardless of the merits of each classification (the issues are mainly of interest to professional ornithologists), for bird-watching purposes I recommend following the first classification used in Roger Tory Peterson's *A Field Guide to the Birds*.

Swans in North America are separated into five species, although only two of these are native continental species (Trumpeter Swan and Whistling Swan). Two others are accidental visitors to North America—Whooper Swan and Bewick's Swan. These two species are encountered very rarely, and are unlikely to be seen by novice birdwatchers. The fifth species, the Mute Swan, is a Eurasian bird that was introduced to many wetlands in parts of the United States (especially city ponds and lakes) where they probably are the most widely observed swans in the country. In a few areas—Massachusetts, Long Island, coastal New Jersey, the northwestern part of Michigan's lower peninsula, and elsewhere—small wild populations of Mute Swans also are established and can be observed with relative ease. Despite the fact that they are not native North American birds, they nevertheless give novice birdwatchers an excellent opportunity to observe the typical appearance of swans and allow them to compare these birds with the general appearance of geese and ducks.

As for our native Trumpeter Swans and Whistling Swans, both are likely to be seen only at specific locations and/or certain seasons. Trumpeter Swans, for example, are threatened birds with a very restricted distribution in the West. Probably no more than about 4,500 to 5,000 individuals survive in all of North America. In itself, that is remarkable because early in this century the species was almost exterminated but was saved by imaginative conservation programs.

Mute Swans, now feral in some parts of the United States.

The most likely places to see Trumpeter Swans in summer are in parts of Alaska, west-central Alberta, the Red Rock Lakes section of northwestern Wyoming, and Malheur National Wildlife Refuge in Oregon, Ruby Lake National Wildlife Refuge in Nevada, Lacreek National Wildlife Refuge in South Dakota, and Turnbull National Wildlife Refuge in Washington. During winter, Trumpeter Swans occur in various locations including Yellowstone National Park and the Centennial Valley. Henry's Fork of the Snake River, not far from Island Park, Idaho, is a particularly important wintering site used by hundreds of the swans, and Red Rock Lakes National Wildlife Refuge also supports major wintering populations of the birds. Thus, if one lives in or visits the correct part of the country, it is easy to see these splendid birds without too much difficulty.

Whistling Swans, the other native North American species, are much more numerous than Trumpeter Swans but, depending upon where one lives, it may not be possible to see these majestic birds.

During the spring and summer breeding season, for example, they nest in the High Arctic of Alaska and Canada—areas that few people have opportunities to visit. During the spring and autumn migrations, however, as well as during winter, when these birds occur in the lower 48 states in sizeable numbers, it is possible to enjoy spectacular views of the large white birds flying overhead, feeding in fields, or resting on bays, rivers, lakes, and other wetland areas. The southern Great Lakes area, the lower Susquehanna River in southern Pennsylvania, and especially Chesapeake Bay are perhaps the best areas to look for these birds, but certain areas in central and southern California and elsewhere also support impressive numbers of the birds as well. Occasionally other locations attract flocks of Whistling Swans where previously they did not occur or were seen only in very small numbers. In mid-March of 1982, for example, more than 1,000 Whistling Swans spent a few hours on the wetlands of the Middle Creek Wildlife Management Area near Lancaster, Pennsylvania, providing birdwatchers with magnificent opportunities to study and enjoy the birds. Public water supply reservoirs also sometimes attract small numbers of Whistling Swans and, therefore, are worthwhile places to check for the presence of these birds during the migration seasons.

Geese form the second broad group of waterfowl which novice birdwatchers will want to learn to recognize and identify if they do not already have the ability to do so. By far, the species with the largest numbers and widest distribution on the continent is the Canada Goose which most people already are able to recognize. Few public wetlands are without at least a few of these birds. Indeed, in many American cities, their numbers have increased dramatically within recent years to the point that severe population explosions exist. Novice birdwatchers certainly will want to learn to instantly recognize this species because it serves as a standard of comparison with other North American geese that might be encountered occasionally or unexpectedly.

Here it is not necessary to discuss each of the five additional native geese species, but several are worth mentioning because they are splendid waterfowl spectacles when seen in large numbers. The Snow Goose is one of these. These birds nest in the High Alaskan and Canadian Arctic in spring and summer, then migrate across much of the United States to reach or return from their wintering grounds along coastal New Jersey, the Chesapeake Bay area (Chincoteague National Wildlife Refuge in Virginia provides excellent viewing opportunities in November and December) southward to coastal North Carolina, the Gulf Coast area, the Puget Sound section of Washington, and a few other scattered locations. To see thousands of these snow white birds with black wingtips is a remarkable sight not soon forgotten. Some of the Snow Geese one observes, however, such as those along the Mississippi River flyway, are so-called "Blue Geese" (a grayish color variation of the white birds), but along the Atlantic coast most are pure white birds. They are very different in appearance from Canada Geese and, therefore, provide birdwatchers with additional reference marks against which other species of geese can be compared and identified.

Ducks form the third very broad group of waterfowl species with which novice birdwatchers must deal. Some, such as Mallards, are so well known to almost everybody that they hardly

Snow Geese on Chincoteague National Wildlife Refuge, Virginia. Photo by Jan Sosik.

An American Black Duck.

need further discussion, but most other species are unfamiliar to beginning birders and will need considerable study. Thus it is important to learn the basic groupings of these birds, the typical habitats in which they are most likely to be observed, and the various field marks (colors and patterns of plumage, types of behavior, and relative abundance) that enable birdwatchers to distinguish one species from all others. These basic groupings already are outlined in field guides which also provide excellent illustrations and text which should enable most novice birdwatchers sooner or later to recognize the various species.

It is well to keep in mind, however, that males among waterfowl species are much more vividly colored than females and, therefore, easier to recognize and identify correctly. An exception is in summer when ducks are molting in their so-called eclipse plumage. Then males tend to resemble females and often appear strikingly different than they do a few months later when they are in full breeding plumage.

A Hooded Merganser.

Finally, one should keep in mind that waterfowl species are popular birds often reared in captivity. Sometimes such birds escape. Therefore there always is the strong probability that exotic or foreign species seen in a seemingly wild setting are not wild visitors from some far distant place but actually only birds that escaped from a private or zoo collection. In addition, waterfowl are notoriously susceptible to crossbreeding. It is not at all unusual to observe hybrids between various species. Thus if one sees an odd-looking duck or goose, and is unable to identify the bird based upon information presented in field guides and other reference books, or if a bird seems to have physical characteristics of two different species, it is very possible that the bird is a hybrid. To rule out the possiblity that the bird is not a foreign species with which you are not familiar, reference to Peter Scott's excellent *A Coloured Key to the Wildfowl of the World* will provide a quick way to see illustrations of all of the world's waterfowl species. Every serious birdwatcher should have a copy of this inexpensive book available at home or in his or her automobile because of its global coverage of waterfowl.

ADDITIONAL READING

Bellrose, F. C.
   1976   *Ducks, Geese & Swans of North America.* Stackpole Books,
          Harrisburg, Pa.
Coman, D. R.
   1944   Ducks Along the Delaware. *Cassinia,* 34: 1–12.
Heintzelman, D. S.
   1963   Diving Times of a Common Goldeneye. *Wilson Bulletin,* 75
          (1): 91.
   1978   *North American Ducks, Geese & Swans.* Winchester Press,
          New York, N. Y.
Heintzelman, D. S. and R. MacClay
   1979   Flock Sizes of Migrating Canada Geese in Eastern Pennsyl-
          vania in Autumn. *Cassina,* 57: 25.
Heintzelman, D. S. and C. J. Newberry
   1964   Some Waterfowl Diving Times. *Wilson Bulletin,* 76 (3): 291.
Johnsgard, P. A.
   1975   *Waterfowl of North America.* Indiana University Press,
          Bloomington, Ind.
Peterson, R. T.
   1980   *A Field Guide to the Birds.* Fourth Edition. Houghton Mifflin
          Co., Boston, Mass.
Sabin, W. B.
   1982   New York State Waterfowl Count, January 1981. *Kingbird,*
          32 (1): 9–15.
Scott, P.
   1968   *A Coloured Key to the Wildfowl of the World.* The Wildfowl
          Trust, Slimbridge, Gloucestershire, England.
Sladen, W. J. L.
   1975   Tireless Voyager the Whistling Swan. *National Geographic,*
          148 (1): 134–147. July issue.

Chapter 6

Projects With Birds of Prey

Watching migrating hawks and other diurnal birds of prey from lookouts or concentration areas in autumn or spring, or from roadsides or other concentration areas at other seasons of the year, now is one of the glamour specialties of bird watching. Tens of thousands of birdwatchers visit hawk lookouts, Bald Eagle concentration areas, or roadside viewing areas in the United States and Canada annually for a day or weekend of relaxation and hawk watching. A good deal of information on this topic now is published in a series of my books including *Autumn Hawk Flights, A Guide to Hawk Watching in North America,* and *Hawks and Owls of North America.* Additional related information appears in other well-known books including Broun's *Hawks Aloft,* Brett and Nagy's *Feathers in the Wind,* Harwood's *The View from Hawk Mountain,* and various regional publications. These are the essential references one uses to learn about recreational hawk watching in North America. In addition, much special literature also is published in ornithological periodicals and newsletters issued by various raptor study organizations.

Some aspects of hawk watching, however, tend to receive much less public attention and consideration, although they lend themselves readily to projects for hawk watchers. Some are discussed here to encourage persons to act upon these often neglected aspects of raptor watching, promotion, and conservation.

RAPTOR REFUGES

Several years ago, in *Hawks and Owls of North America*, I pointed out that much more effort should be placed on the creation or establishment of refuges for birds of prey in North America. Even today, relatively few refuges exist specifically to protect and preserve raptor habitat and the birds of prey that live there. Yet there are many sites along migration routes, in wintering

Recreational hawk watchers on the lookout at Bake Oven Knob, Pennsylvania.

A migrating Sharp-shinned Hawk.

areas, or in breeding areas that might make valuable raptor refuges. Clearly, opportunities are available for bird clubs, nature clubs, government agencies, and private citizens to help create raptor refuges or reserves. Indeed, the time is ripe all across North America for concerned persons to exhibit imagination and skill in raptor refuge establishment! By protecting areas where birds of prey are common, it is unlikely that future and expensive endangered species programs will be needed.

American Kestrels provide an excellent example of a species particularly well suited to refuge establishment. These small falcons readily accept nest boxes as breeding sites, in addition to using natural openings and cavities in trees for the same purposes. In addition, the birds often live on farms where they feed largely upon small rodents and insects. Not infrequently, therefore, farmers are eager to cooperate with hawk watchers and allow the placement of American Kestrel nest boxes on their property. The net result is the creation of a network of refuges for these birds.

Most farmers who participate in the establishment of kestrel refuges also welcome all birds of prey because they understand that these birds are ecologically important.

Ospreys provide another example of a spectacular raptor that can benefit from the creation of special refuges to protect and preserve its nesting grounds from needless disturbance or destruction. In fact, some such refuges already exist. One is Gardiners Island off the tip of Long Island. Here, prior to the destructive impact of DDT upon the reproduction of these fine birds, hundreds of nests successfully produced young. Indeed, the Osprey colony on Gardiners Island was perhaps the largest of its kind found anywhere in the world. Today, despite the decline in numbers of this species, some birds still nest on the island and there is hope that many more again will do so in the future as the chemicals gradually disappear from the environment. Thus it is important that sites that are particularly suited to the needs of Ospreys and have a long history of successful use prior to the pesticide era are protected and preserved, so that future generations of these birds can eventually establish themselves there again.

In fact, there are many locations in the United States where Ospreys still nest. Local bird clubs and birdwatchers should seek the cooperation of the owners of the property on which such nests are located in an effort to establish either public or private Osprey refuges.

In other cases, erection of tall poles with platforms on the top, along the shorelines of reservoirs and other large lakes—especially if such locations are closed to public entrance—might in time lure Ospreys as breeding birds. However, an adequate supply of fish must be present nearby to serve as the food supply for the birds. Nevertheless, where such favorable conditions occur, birdwatchers could possibly aid local Osprey populations by discussing such projects with owners of reservoirs and other lakes. In some instances government agencies, utilities, or other organizations are willing to lend technical or financial support in return for the public relations exposure they receive for their efforts. Perhaps their motives are less than ideal, but if the end result aids Ospreys, the projects are worthwhile.

Refuges for nesting Ospreys are needed in many areas of the United States. Bird-watchers can play important roles in helping to create such refuges.

There are, of course, other opportunities for the creation of refuges for raptors. Field surveys can be employed to locate and identify such sites and gather basic background data on their ornithological and ecological importance. Then, armed with such information, organized efforts can be made by concerned individuals to achieve refuge status for such locations either by purchase, lease, cooperative agreement, or other means. Some such efforts are underway or completed already for Bald Eagles by the Nature Conservancy, National Wildlife Federation, Eagle Valley Environmentalists, and others. But much remains to be done, with plenty of opportunities open to all who are concerned about the future survival of birds of prey. For example, special efforts might be made to create refuges for colonies of Burrowing Owls. Other species of owls also are worthy of enjoying refuge status, although few such owl refuges currently exist in North America.

NATIONAL HAWK LOOKOUT SURVEY

In 1977, in an article published in the American Birding Association's magazine *Birding*, I pointed out that it is highly desirable to conduct a national inventory of hawk migration lookouts so that the scientific, conservation, and educational importance of these sites will not accidentally be overlooked in regional and other planning programs. It is important, I feel, that such sites be preserved and protected as unique research, conservation-education, and recreation locations.

The American Birding Association supports this effort but, to date, few new site write-ups have appeared in *Birding*. Here, then, is a splendid opportunity for hawk watchers and other birders to aid raptor conservation and enjoy the adventure of hawk watching. One can explore new areas, seeking important new migration lookouts never known previously to birdwatchers. Basic ornithological information can be gathered on the species and temporal composition of the hawk flights observed passing the new sites, and one can publicize basic details about the sites. By this process one not only becomes an explorer and birdwatcher but one also makes a lasting contribution to future generations of hawk watchers. Much field exploration is needed still to discover all the productive hawk lookouts in the East, whereas in the West almost nothing is known about hawk migrations, although there is a recent surge of interest in western hawk watching by limited numbers of people.

Birdwatchers interested in this type of exploratory hawk watching, probing the unexplored frontiers of bird watching, will find *A Guide to Hawk Watching in North America* a model after which site write-ups can be prepared. Particular note should be made of the fact that I rate each lookout quantitatively based upon standards set forth in lookout rating scales contained in the preface of that book. Thus all lookouts are directly comparable insofar as the magnitude of the hawk flights passing each is concerned. I urge other hawk watchers, beginners and old pros, to use these rating scales to evaluate the importance of any new lookouts being studied.

When using the hawks per hour rating scale, the average number of hawks observed per hour refers to the time the lookout

Hawks Per Hour Rating Scale

Lookout Rating	Average Number of Hawks Observed Per Hour
Poor	0 to 11
Fair	12 to 22
Good	23 to 33
Excellent	34 or more

Hawks Per Day Rating Scale

Lookout Rating	Average Number of Hawks Observed Per Day
Poor	0 to 46
Fair	47 to 92
Good	93 to 138
Excellent	139 or more

Source: *A Guide to Hawk Watching in North America.*

itself is being used. Thus a lookout in operation for eight hours with six observers present, or a lookout in operation for eight hours with one observer present, both result in eight lookout hours. In short, the number of observers present at a lookout does not influence the number of hours of operation determined for a given lookout.

In a similar manner, an arbitrary use of the category "day" also is assigned when determining the number of days a lookout is in operation. For purposes here, the term "day" applies to a given date regardless of the number of hours the lookout is being used on that date.

HAWK MIGRATION STUDIES

Within recent years recreational hawk watching has developed into a major branch of bird watching. As a result, tens of thousands of people now use hundreds of hawk lookouts in the East, and a few in the West, during autumn in an effort to observe large flights of migrating diurnal birds of prey. Spring hawk watching, however, is much less developed as a branch of bird watching. Nevertheless there are some excellent spring hawk lookouts in constant use, such as Braddock Bay State Park and Derby Hill along the southern shore of Lake Ontario in upstate New York. At Braddock Bay, for example, hawk watcher Laura Moon and a team of dedicated observers cover the lookout daily for about three months every spring and count between 25,000 and 30,000 hawks migrating northward past the spot.

Some spring and autumn hawk watchers also engage in various research projects dealing with many aspects of hawk migrations, both for pleasure and to try to advance knowledge of these migrations. Such research by amateur hawk watchers is to be encouraged. A few suggestions for worthwhile hawk migration projects therefore are presented here.

Hawk watchers at Braddock Bay, New York. Photo by Dave Spier.

To some extent, the seasonal patterns of migration exhibited by various raptors varies slightly from site to site. Thus it is worthwhile to chart the variations, species by species and week by week, to define them at different sites. There are various ways this can be done. One is to determine the total number of a species counted for each week during the entire season or period of the study, then calculate the percentage that each weekly total represents compared with the total count for the study period. This information then can be depicted in a bar graph showing the weekly variations in numbers of the species observed. The result provides a seasonal picture of the peak migration periods for the species at the site being studied.

It also is worthwhile to note the exact time (use standard time) when rare or endangered raptors such as eagles, Rough-legged Hawks, and Peregrine Falcons pass a lookout. After an adequate number of sightings are available—20 or more years of such information is ideal—it is possible to organize the data into one-hour intervals to look for obvious trends in daily rhythms or noon lulls. I conducted just such a study of daily rhythms of Golden Eagles and Bald Eagles passing Bake Oven Knob, Pennsylvania, between 1961 and 1981. To gather the necessary information, 1,288 days (7,914 hours) were spent on the lookouts by myself and several associates. We counted 450 Golden Eagles and 326 Bald Eagles. When this information was organized into the hours when the birds were seen, it became clear that Golden Eagles passed the Knob in largest numbers between one and two o'clock in the afternoon, but anytime between nine o'clock in the morning and four o'clock in the afternoon could produce reasonable possibilities of seeing an eagle. However, at Bake Oven Knob the rumor passed among some hawk watchers that eagles pass late in the day was not correct. Bald Eagles, on the other hand, occurred in largest numbers between noon and one o'clock in the afternoon, but the period between ten o'clock in the morning and three o'clock in the afternoon tended to produce reasonable numbers of our national bird. As with Golden Eagles, however, there was little opportunity to observe Bald Eagles after four o'clock in the afternoon at this site.

Age ratio data for migrating birds of prey also is useful and important information, although relatively little information of this type is available. Here, then, is an excellent opportunity to gather information of use to bird population students and raptor conservationists. For some species, such as eagles, it is relatively easy to determine approximate ages of the birds being observed and to note that information in field notes. I present criteria for determining eagle age classes in *A Guide to Hawk Watching in North America*. At Bake Oven Knob, for example, my associates and I have been doing just that for more than two decades, and the eagle age ratio data we have developed over the years are a major source of reference information for Golden Eagles and Bald Eagles in the East. It is particularly interesting that Bald Eagles showed serious reductions in the ratio of immatures to adult birds during the years when DDT and other pesticides were used widely and in an unrestricted manner, whereas Golden Eagles during that same period tended to show little or no reduction in the number of immatures in their population. But within recent years, Bald Eagles migrating past Bake Oven Knob are showing marked improvement in the numbers of immatures seen. Apparently Bald Eagles (like Peregrine Falcons and other birds associated with aquatic habitats in their breeding season) reflected pesticide pollution in their habitat, whereas Golden Eagles tended to reflect much less impact of pesticides in their habitat since they lived in habitats in mountains or otherwise largely away from water and the food they consumed was largely nonaquatic and not very contaminated by DDT.

Carefully coordinated studies of hawk migrations passing two or more closely located lookouts also are most worthwhile because such studies can help to define the role of geography upon the migration patterns of various raptors. A variety of such close-site studies conducted in the past are reported in *Autumn Hawk Flights*, whereas more recent studies of this type are discussed in various publications issued by the Hawk Migration Association of North America, the Vermont Institute of Science, and other organizations. To conduct such field studies requires very careful record keeping at the lookouts—usually by thirty- or sixty-minute intervals throughout each day of the study.

Relatively few studies have been made on the correlation of surface wind directions and speeds on the manner in which hawks migrate past lookouts. Such studies, therefore, also are worthwhile. Do different species of hawks, eagles, and falcons use one side of the mountain or the other under different wind speeds and/or directions? How does such local migration behavior compare with the same species and weather conditions at other lookouts? Can some general trends or patterns be detected after studies of this type are completed?

Still another aspect of hawk migrations that has received very limited study is the role of human visual or other limitations in securing accurate counts of hawks migrating past a lookout. Can one person make more accurate counts of raptors than another with equal field experience? How important is human visual acuity? How important is hawk-watching experience? And, how important is optical equipment of various types?

The influence of large bodies of open water upon the routes used by migrating hawks and other diurnal birds of prey has been a subject of considerable interest to hawk watchers and ornithologists for decades. Although some raptors such as Ospreys and Peregrine Falcons readily migrate over large expanses of open water, other species such as Broad-winged Hawks apparently do so only rarely and unsuccessfully. Much remains to be learned about these over-the-water hawk migrations, however, thus providing plenty of opportunities for hawk watchers and birdwatchers to study the problem as opportunities develop. For the most part, observations with binoculars and telescopes are the techniques generally used to gather information on over-the-water hawk migrations. In the future, however, radar and other techniques might provide more comprehensive information on the problem. These advanced techniques probably will be used only by professional ornithologists associated with universities or other institutions. Nevertheless, the direct visual observations of recreational hawk watchers and other birdwatchers who happen to observe raptors migrating over open bodies of water such as the Great Lakes or the Gulf of Maine or Mexico still will provide much needed and most valuable evidence to the hawk-watching community. Clearly, these and similar problems can lead to many fascinating field projects for birdwatchers.

NATIONAL HAWK WATCHING WEEK

During the last century, and well into this one, countless numbers of birds of prey were shot, trapped, or poisoned by hunters,

Variations in human visual acuity can be a subject of study for hawk watchers.

Much remains to be learned about over-the-water migrations of some raptors including Broad-winged Hawks.

ranchers, farmers, game managers, sportsmen and other persons in the belief that such "control" (meaning extermination) of predatory birds would benefit hunting, farming, and other economic or recreational interests. That such beliefs were incorrect is now well documented in a vast amount of scientific literature dealing with the ecology, biology, and economies of birds of prey. It is known now that raptors are vital ecological components of the wildlife communities and ecosystems in which they live. They help to remove weak, sick, diseased, or occasionally overabundant numbers of wildlife from ecosystems. Thus birds of prey are major components of the so-called balance of nature.

Today public attitudes regarding birds of prey are changing from one of hatred and lack of understanding to one of appreciation and understanding. For example, upwards of 150,000 people now actively participate in recreational hawk watching every autumn (and in spring at a few locations) at migration lookouts located on major raptor flyways scattered from California to Maine, and from Minnesota to Florida and Texas. In addition, millions of birdwatchers, nature photographers, and other outdoor enthusiasts also watch hawks and other birds of prey occasionally as opportunities occur. The Age of Hawk Watching has arrived, and Pennsylvania is a major center of that activity.

Much of this activity is recreational in nature, but a good deal of serious scientific research also is being conducted on hawk migrations and other aspects of birds of prey. In addition, each year a growing number of public schools (chiefly fifth and sixth grade classes) take students on day-long field trips to major hawk lookouts in Pennsylvania (Bake Oven Knob and Hawk Mountain often are visited), New Hampshire, and other states. Thus the study of hawk migrations, and birds of prey in general, is part of the science curricula in some school districts.

Additional support for the importance of hawk watching and birds of prey, along with the sites from which hawk watching is

Recreational hawk watching now is a major branch of bird watching. These hawk watchers are at Derby Hill, New York.

done, resulted in 1978 in two levels of Pennsylvania government providing recognition of the international significance of the Kittatinny Ridge (Blue Mountain) as a major autumn migration route for diurnal birds of prey. In Lehigh County, the executive issued a resolution (his first) designating the Lehigh County section of the Kittatinny Ridge as the Lehigh County Raptor Migration Area. Shortly thereafter, the Pennsylvania Game Commission accepted my recommendation and designated the entire length of the Kittatinny Ridge (about 150 miles of mountain between Delaware Water Gap and Carlisle) as the Kittatinny Ridge Birds of Prey Natural Area.

Despite these advances in raptor conservation and promotion, large numbers of Americans still do not know much (if anything) about birds of prey and their ecological and aesthetic importance. In order to focus additional public attention on birds of prey, early in 1978 I originated the idea for, and proposed to the Congress of the United States, that Congress establish an annual

Student hawk watchers recording data at Bake Oven Knob, Pennsylvania.

A student hawk watcher in action at Bake Oven Knob, Pennsylvania.

National Hawk Watching Week to be held the first full week of each October. The purpose of the annual observance is to provide wildlife conservationists with a unique and valuable public relations tool to be used with skill and imagination to promote public interest in and protection of birds of prey. By having a week set aside each year for this purpose, birdwatchers, bird clubs, and others concerned with advancing wildlife conservation have a built-in wedge into the news media. Thus conservationists can distribute various raptor conservation messages via radio, television, newspapers, magazines, and lectures. They can encourage public schools to add raptor materials to their curricula during that week (and at other times during the school year) to make certain that students receive some basic instruction about the ecological importance of raptors.

On May 1, 1979, a House Joint Resolution providing for a National Hawk Watching Week was introduced into the House of Representatives, and on May 3, 1979, an identical Senate Joint

A kettle (flock) of migrating Broad-winged Hawks.

Resolution was introduced into the United States Senate. Numerous conservation organizations and bird clubs, as well as individuals and some schools, supported the effort with letters to their representatives. To date, however, the resolution has not come out of committee in the House of Representatives. It is time that all American birdwatchers and conservationists write their Congressmen and ask that this resolution be released and voted upon. National Hawk Watching Week is a tool we need and can use effectively to promote raptor conservation in the United States. Thus I would urge all readers to write to their Congressmen and seek *cosponsorship* of the resolution without delay.

NATIONAL BALD EAGLE DAY

In 1982, Congress passed a resolution providing for the celebration of National Bald Eagle Day in honor of our national bird and Americans celebrated the event in June. This can be a very worthwhile educational event calling the national bird and its fight for survival to the attention of all Americans; it also can have a negative effect upon some eagles. These birds are unusually sensitive to human disturbance and can be forced to leave areas if people approach them within about one-quarter mile. It is important, therefore, that Bald Eagles be observed only from safe distances or the positive impact that National Bald Eagle Day might have can be offset by unintended damage or disturbance to the birds.

EAGLE AWARENESS WEEK

In 1980, the Governor of Arkansas proclaimed an Eagle Awareness Week, the purpose of which was to better inform citizens of the state about Bald Eagles. Similar programs also would be worthwhile in other states, keeping in mind the approach restrictions mentioned earlier, especially where considerable numbers of eagles occur and offer citizens opportunities for observation. Eagle Awareness Week, therefore, is a public relations and educational tool that should be used by raptor conservationists, educators, wildlife conservation agents, and others concerned

The Bald Eagle is the national bird of the United States of America, and the subject of National Bald Eagle Day. Photo by U. S. Fish and Wildlife Service.

about the welfare of eagles and the advancement of wildlife educational programs.

STATE HAWK WATCHING WEEK

Whereas federal action on National Hawk Watching Week is pending, Pennsylvania already has taken the lead and established its own Hawk Watching Week in 1979, 1980, 1981, and 1982 thanks to Governor Dick Thornburgh's willingness to accept my suggestion that he issue a proclamation designating such an event early in October. Largely promotional in nature and a tool to be used by Pennsylvania raptor and hawk-watching enthusiasts to promote raptor understanding and conservation in the state, it also puts the Governor on record as supporting wise use of birds of prey via observation and appreciation—this in a state formerly notorious for allowing massive shooting of migrating hawks.

There is no reason why other states can't also designate Hawk Watching Weeks and thus follow Pennsylvania's leadership in gaining another useful conservation tool.

STATE RAPTOR CONFERENCES

Each state and Canadian province has its own peculiar problems and opportunities to deal with the conservation of birds of prey. All too frequently, however, raptor enthusiasts and other persons interested in raptors have failed to unite in their concerns and efforts to develop effective and unique state raptor conservation programs.

One effective and enjoyable way to solve the problem is to hold one- or two-day state raptor conferences during which nontechnical discussions of raptor promotion and education, research, management, and governmental action can be presented by experts with audience participation. On June 14, 1980, for example, the Pennsylvania chapter of the Sierra Club sponsored a raptor conference of this type with 175 amateur and professional raptor enthusiasts attending. The result was informative and educational for everyone and may lead to advances in the protection and conservation of birds of prey in Pennsylvania.

Basic topics presented at Pennsylvania Raptor Conference 1980 were divided into four broad categories—promotion and education, pure research, management, and governmental action. Within each a variety of specific subjects were discussed by various persons. While other state raptor conferences might select other formats, the one used in Pennsylvania is useful and can serve as a model upon which interested persons elsewhere can develop their own state conferences.

ROADSIDE RAPTOR COUNTS

Although hawk watching from the many fine lookouts in the United States still remains the most commonly employed form of watching birds of prey, other types of raptor viewing also are used to a lesser extent. Perhaps the most easy-to-use of these is watching birds of prey in areas adjacent to roads. Thus one merely

PROCLAMATION

HAWK WATCHING WEEK
OCTOBER 3 - 9, 1982

Nature lovers in Pennsylvania and across the country enjoy observing the flight of the hawk, an attractive bird which helps maintain the delicate balance of nature and preserve our environment.

Hawk watching has become an increasingly popular activity in the Commonwealth, and we are fortunate to have some of the world's best hawk migration outlooks, making us a keystone state for hawk watching. The annual autumn hawk migration gives citizens a fine opportunity to observe and photograph these magnificent birds. Bake Oven Knob, Hawk Mountain and other Pennsylvania mountains have become popular meccas for bird watching enthusiasts. The Pennsylvania Game Commission has also designated nearly 150 miles of the Kittatinny Ridge mountaintop as the Kittatinny Birds of Prey Natural Area.

Therefore, I, Dick Thornburgh, Governor of the Commonwealth of Pennsylvania, do hereby proclaim October 3 - 9, 1982 as HAWK WATCHING WEEK in Pennsylvania. I hope that all Pennsylvanians will take advantage of the great opportunities to observe the beauty of hawks in flight in the Keystone State -- one of the best viewing areas in the world.

GIVEN under my hand and the Seal of the Governor, at the City of Harrisburg, this second day of July in the year of our Lord one thousand nine hundred and eighty-two, and of the Commonwealth the two hundred and sixth.

Dick Thornburgh
Governor

The 1982 Hawk Watching Week proclamation issued by Pennsylvania Governor Dick Thornburgh.

selects a particular road, or series of roads, which form a route that is used repeatedly over a period of one year or longer. Some observers run their routes as frequently as once each week, but often a raptor survey is made once per month. In any case, all of the birds of prey observed perched or in flight along both sides of the route are recorded in notebooks along with related data on weather conditions, time of day the census is made, date, and other vital information.

Over a period of time, hopefully several years, such roadside raptor counts can provide enthusiasts with a very crude index of the relative abundance of various species of birds of prey in the area. Generally those species that prefer open country—vultures, soaring hawks, some eagles, and certain falcons—are the most likely to be seen along the sides of roads, whereas shy woodland species like the accipiters rarely are noted. This places a bias in the counts, but if one is aware of these limitations, any conclusions drawn from roadside raptor counts do not pretend to reflect the status of Cooper's Hawks or other accipiters.

MIDWINTER BALD EAGLE SURVEY

In 1979, the National Wildlife Federation began a midwinter survey of Bald Eagles in each of the lower 48 states in an effort to try to determine how many eagles were present in the contiguous states. This survey now is an annual event and offers opportunities to people interested in eagles to seek their presence in a person's home area, while at the same time adding data to a worthwhile project. Full details on the survey, and how one may participate, are available from the National Wildlife Federation, 1412 Sixteenth St., N. W., Washington, D. C. 20036.

EAGLE AGE RATIOS

In those sections of the United States and Canada where Golden Eagles and/or Bald Eagles occur in considerable numbers, it is possible to gather enough information on the approximate age ratios of these birds to effectively monitor the health of local eagle populations. Information of this type, when collected for many

Rough-legged Hawks sometimes are seen when roadside raptor counts are conducted. Photo by Harry Goldman.

years or decades, is extremely desirable and provides important comparative background information against which future changes in the age structure of eagle populations can be measured and evaluated. *A Guide to Hawk Watching in North America* is a particularly helpful field reference for persons trying to determine the approximate ages of eagles.

AMERICAN KESTREL NEST BOX TRAILS

As mentioned earlier in this chapter, American Kestrels readily accept and use nest boxes as substitutes for natural nest sites, thus providing birdwatchers and raptor enthusiasts with excellent opportunities to develop important and effective raptor conservation projects. The organization, known as Kestrel Karetakers, attempts to coordinate the development and operation of American Kestrel nest box trails throughout the United States.

Birdwatchers interested in establishing an American Kestrel

Nest box trails for American Kestrels are excellent conservation projects. Photo by Harry Goldman.

nest box trail should keep in mind the following basic requirements for the successful operation of such a project.

1. Select open agricultural areas, or open fields adjacent to wooded areas, to place nest boxes.

2. Place boxes facing south or west and at least twenty feet above the ground. The supporting structure can be a tree or other pole. Even the side of a barn can be used.

3. Construct boxes 11 inches deep, 11 inches wide, and 12 inches high.

4. Put an entrance opening at the top of the front of the box. Make the opening rounded or oval and about 3 inches wide and 4 inches high with rounded corners.

5. Put several drainage holes through the bottom of the box.

6. Allow a small air space for ventilation between the top of the box and the top of each side.

7. Place a small perch *inside* the box below the entrance hole. This allows nestlings to look outside.

8. Put a layer of sawdust or wood shavings on the bottom of the box to allow the female to deposit her eggs on a soft surface.

9. Remove old nesting debris from the inside of the box after the completion of each nesting season. November or December is a good time to clean boxes.

10. Do not disturb nest boxes occupied by breeding American Kestrels unless ornithological research is being conducted. Observe activities at nest boxes only from a safe distance through binoculars or a telescope. This will help to keep predators away from occupied nest boxes and increase the chances of successful nesting efforts by the falcons.

AMERICAN KESTREL SEX RATIOS

Because American Kestrels are distributed widely in North America and males and females can be distinguished easily on the basis of the coloration of their plumage, these small falcons provide abundant and excellent opportunities to determine sex ratios of local kestrel populations. Relatively few field studies of this type have been conducted, however, thus making studies of American Kestrel sex ratios most worthwhile projects in which birdwatchers can participate and help to gather useful scientific information.

REGIONAL RAPTOR CENTERS

An important new trend in raptor conservation efforts is the creation of regional raptor centers where a variety of services are provided by trained professional raptor biologists and amateur volunteers.

At the University of North Carolina at Charlotte, for example, Dr. Richard D. Brown is leading the development of the Carolina Raptor Rehabilitation and Research Center which deals with raptor rehabilitation, research, conservation, and education. In addition to graduate students, some thirty volunteers assist in the work of the center which engages in such varied projects as rehabilitating injured Bald Eagles, hacking Golden Eagles and Ospreys, developing educational publications and other materials, and even visiting day-care centers for small children. Similar regional raptor centers in other parts of the country could be equally valuable and interested birdwatchers might wish to explore the possibility of their establishment.

Another example of a particularly worthwhile regional raptor center is located in St. Paul, Minnesota. There the Raptor Research and Rehabilitation Center is part of the University of Minnesota's College of Veterinary Medicine. Drs. Gary Duke and Pat Redig lead the program which conducts veterinary research on the care and treatment of raptors, offers rehabilitation of these birds, trains veterinary students to treat and work with birds of prey, and provides the public with an information and education service. Research into the proper veterinary care of raptors is an especially important part of this Minnesota center's work because new methods and techniques of treatment developed there eventually may be used at other similar regional raptor centers.

SPECIAL RAPTOR COURSES

Within relatively recent years several special educational courses dealing with birds of prey have been developed by various persons and presented to selected groups of people. In 1968, for example, I developed a special one-day course dealing with raptor identification, ecology, and conservation as part of my curatorial duties at the William Penn Memorial Museum in Harrisburg, Pennsylvania. The course then was presented to a class of men undergoing training as new game protectors for the Pennsylvania Game Commission. Several years later, when I was employed by the New Jersey State Museum, a similar course was presented to New Jersey's wildlife conservation officers. Most of the people taking these courses knew relatively little about birds of prey and, therefore, found the information presented most helpful. Not only did they have opportunities to handle museum specimens of the various species native to each state and learn to identify them, but they also looked at motion pictures dealing with hawk migrations and received additional information about other aspects of raptor conservation.

Within recent years several middle schools in Lehigh and Carbon counties in eastern Pennsylvania, as well as in several other states, have introduced teaching units on birds of prey (including hawk migrations and hawk watching) into their science curricula. Until 1979, however, formal in-service training for teachers presenting this material has not been available. It was then that I developed and taught a two-credit (thirty contact hours) course entitled "Introduction to Hawk Watching for Elementary and Secondary Teachers" as part of the course offerings of the Carbon-Lehigh Intermediate Unit. More than twenty public school teachers completed the course.

This course was designed to provide a basic review of autumn and spring hawk watching. Topics included hawk identification, hawk migrations and weather, history of hawk watching, a survey of important hawk lookouts now in use, hawk ecology, endangered hawks, and winter and summer hawk watching. Fifteen hours were spent in the classroom; the other fifteen hours consisted of two field trips to Bake Oven Knob in Lehigh County. The basic text used during the course was *A Guide to Hawk Watching in North America*. A great deal of additional handout material was used during the course.

Presentation of such a course could be a most worthwhile project elsewhere by other experienced hawk watchers working in cooperation with regional school officials. Based upon our experience with this course and the comments and recommendations of the teachers taking the course, some specific recommendations can be made. First, the course can be shortened to a one-credit course containing fifteen contact hours. Three of those hours (the first meeting, in a classroom) could deal with hawk identification using slides, 16mm motion pictures, and other visual aids. The rest of the course could consist of three field trips to hawk lookouts, each field trip lasting four hours. During the field trips, some of the information originally presented in formal classroom situations could be presented informally on the lookouts during the wait for hawks to appear. This would provide a more relaxed atmosphere and probably be more effective than the formal presentation.

During the past few years the Raptor Information Center of the National Wildlife Federation also developed several raptor short courses for state wildlife officers and others. Additional information on the availability of these courses may be secured from the Center at the National Wildlife Federation, 1412 16th St., N. W., Washington, D. C. 20036.

On the other hand, not all raptor courses need to be short courses. Sometimes it is desirable to present more details (nontechnical), perhaps as noncredit continuing education offerings at a local community college. The original course for teachers that I developed could be used in community colleges. It could introduce local citizens to recreational hawk watching and provide them with the basics necessary to develop an understanding and appreciation of the spectacular hawk migrations that occur in eastern North America in autumn (and spring at a few locations). Details of my teacher's course follow, with emphasis on Kittatinny Ridge hawk flights in autumn in eastern Pennsylvania.

There were four classroom meetings each lasting three hours and two field trips to a local hawk lookout each lasting four hours. Topics presented in the classroom were well organized around specific topics. Field trips, however, were much more informal and information presented depended upon which birds passed the lookouts and the questions class participants asked.

The first classroom meeting explained the basics of flight identification of eastern hawks, especially species that pass the hawk migration lookouts regularly. Field guides such as Roger Tory Peterson's *A Field Guide to the Birds* and my own *A Guide to Hawk Watching in North America* served as texts. In addition, I used various 35mm Kodachrome slides of hawks in flight to show important field marks and flight characteristics.

Before I showed slides or made detailed reference to plates in field guides, however, I presented on the blackboard a more or less standard classification of eastern hawks so that students learned to recognize basic groups of raptors such as vultures, accipiters, buteos, eagles, harriers, Ospreys, and falcons. As I briefly discussed these groups, students had an opportunity to become familiar with the names of the various species likely to be seen on field trips. This classification is outlined in the following way.

Family Cathartidae: New World Vultures
      Genus *Cathartes*: Turkey Vulture
      Genus *Coragyps*: Black Vulture
Family Pandionidae: Osprey
      Genus *Pandion*: Osprey
Family Accipitridae: Hawks, Eagles, Harriers, Etc.
    Subfamily Accipitrinae: Bird Hawks
      Genus *Accipiter*: Northern Goshawk
                 Sharp-shinned Hawk
                 Cooper's Hawk
    Subfamily Buteoninae: Hawks and Eagles
      Genus *Buteo*: Red-tailed Hawk
               Red-shouldered Hawk
               Broad-winged Hawk
               Rough-legged Hawk
      Genus *Aquila*: Golden Eagle
      Genus *Haliaeetus*: Bald Eagle
    Subfamily Circinae: Harriers
      Genus *Circus*: Northern Harrier (Marsh Hawk)
Family Falconidae: Caracaras and Falcons
      Genus *Falco*: Peregrine Falcon
              Merlin
              American Kestrel (Sparrow Hawk)

After the initial discussion of the classification of groups of birds of prey, I returned to the beginning of the classification (the vultures) and discussed each species in depth, including its major field marks and flight style characteristics. Identification plates in field guides, and 35mm slides of birds in flight, augmented the discussion. Asking of questions was encouraged, and information was repeated when necessary. In addition, comparisons of similar species were made so that students would be aware of those birds that tend to cause difficulty for many people in respect to their identification—Cooper's Hawks, immature eagles, and a few others.

At this time, I also pointed out that years (perhaps decades) of field experience, coupled with in-hand examination of specimens in museums and laboratories, are needed before many people develop expert skill in making flight identifications of birds of prey. Thus particular emphasis was placed on training students to recognize and correctly identify the more common hawks of the area.

Finally, a brief portion of the first classroom meeting was devoted to discussing directions for visiting local hawk lookouts, the meeting time for field trips, and necessary equipment to take along such as binoculars, a hat and coat, lunch, proper shoes, and other items. In addition, each student was given sample field data forms on which he or she could keep a record of the birds observed on the field trip. Record keeping was encouraged—not for research purposes, but to enable people to look back upon memorable days in the field and review what they had seen on previous hawk-watching trips.

The second classroom meeting (held after the first field trip was completed) was devoted to the relationships of hawk migrations and weather conditions. The first part of this discussion centered around the role of general weather systems and weather fronts, especially cold fronts and positions of low pressure areas, to eastern Pennsylvania hawk migrations. It was pointed out that studies made by Maurice Broun and others showed a general correlation between notable hawk flights and the passage of cold fronts through the area in which a hawk lookout is located, provided that a low pressure area also was associated slightly ahead and north of the cold front. These general weather conditions often tend to trigger hawk flights a day or two after the weather systems pass across an area. Thus use of newspaper and television weather maps can sometimes be helpful tools to make rough predictions of good hawk flights.

In addition to a discussion of general weather conditions, particular attention also was given to the relationship of surface winds and deflective updrafts to numbers of hawks observed passing hawk lookouts such as Bake Oven Knob and Hawk Mountain, Pennsylvania—the two lookouts most likely to be used in the area. Persons developing a similar course for other sections of the United States or Canada, of course, should select information related to hawk lookouts in their particular areas. The importance of northwest winds to large flights of hawks generally was detailed. So, too, was the importance of thermal formation and use by Broad-winged Hawks, since this species is highly dependent upon thermals in order to complete its long distance migrations from North America to Central and South America, and the sight of hundreds of Broad-wings milling within a thermal is one of the highlights of any hawk watching trip in September. To some extent, wind speed and its relationship to hawk flights also was noted.

Finally the temporal factor of the autumn hawk flights along the Kittatinny Ridge was discussed. A general discussion of the periods during the autumn when each species appears in largest numbers was outlined. In particular, it was indicated that Broad-winged Hawks occur in largest numbers during September with their peak flights passing the eastern Pennsylvania hawk lookouts in the middle of the month. Then follow large flights of Sharp-shinned Hawks in late September and early to mid-October. Red-tailed Hawks then begin to build to their peak numbers in late October and early to mid-November. Other species, such as Bald Eagles, are seen mostly from late August through September, whereas Golden Eagles tend to occur mainly from mid-October to the end of November or early December. Ospreys pass in largest numbers during September, especially the third week of that month. Some details of the temporal aspect of the migration periods of other species seen passing the lookouts also were mentioned briefly.

This seasonal aspect of the migrations is important for several

An Osprey migrating on strong northwest winds along the Kittatinny Ridge in eastern Pennsylvania.

reasons. First, by knowing when a species is most likely to occur it helps to make possible eliminations of unlikely species during the identification process—although there always can be early, late, or unexpected species to keep skilled hawkwatchers on their toes. Secondly, a knowledge of the temporal aspect of autumn hawk migrations also allows one to select the period most likely to result in the observation of a particular species. For example, if one wishes to observe Golden Eagles at Bake Oven Knob or Hawk Mountain, the most likely period to do so is from mid-October to the end of the fall season late in November. In comparison, Bald Eagles appear much earlier in the season.

The essential reference books for this part of the course were Maurice Broun's *Hawks Aloft* and my own *Autumn Hawk Flights: The Migrations in Eastern North America.* Both books were widely available in local public and college libraries, which permitted the more serious and dedicated students to borrow copies and continue a more detailed study of the topic.

Raptor ecology was the subject of the third classroom meeting. The first part of this class was devoted to a nontechnical examination of food habits of selected raptor species including Northern Goshawks, Cooper's Hawks, Red-tailed Hawks, Golden and Bald Eagles, Ospreys, and American Kestrels. Then followed discussions of food chains and food webs and the overall role of birds of prey in wildlife communities. Selected references for this part of the course included my own *Hawks and Owls of North America* along with John B. May's *The Hawks of North America*, Ian Newton's *Population Ecology of Raptors*, and various information published in ornithological journals.

The final classroom meeting was devoted to a discussion of the history of hawk shooting, hawk protection, hawk watching, and hawk conservation in North America, including some of the techniques currently in use to aid these birds. Particular emphasis was placed on the history of raptor conservation in Pennsylvania, extending back as far as 1819–1839 when bounties were paid on predators by officials of Lehigh County. Thus a century and one-half of raptor history was discussed. A special part of this discussion centered around the hawk shooting that formerly occurred at Bake Oven Knob and Hawk Mountain, the reasons why Hawk Mountain was established as the world's first refuge for birds of prey, and the role of Maurice and Irma Broun in stopping hawk shooting in Pennsylvania and building Hawk Mountain into the internationally recognized wildlife refuge it is today. Enactment of federal legislation providing for raptor protection also was discussed, as was the growth of recreational hawk watching as a major branch of general bird watching.

This particular classroom meeting allowed the use of a wide variety of visual aids, including enlargements of some of the old photographs of dead hawks littering the ground at Hawk Mountain prior to its creation as a wildlife sanctuary, photographs of hawk shooters in their gunning blinds, pictures of dead hawks at Bake Oven Knob, and related materials.

I also read short passages from Maurice Broun's *Hawks Aloft*, especially sections that described his early and difficult efforts to stop gunners from killing hawks at Hawk Mountain in 1934 just after its creation. I considered it important that recreational hawk-watchers, visiting hawk lookouts today, understand that threats were made on the lives of Maurice Broun and others in their early attempts to stop hawk shooting at Hawk Mountain, and that their success in stopping the killing of these birds and establishing a unique wildlife sanctuary was as much a matter of good fortune as skill. There were times in those years when the entire effort could have ended in disaster and the conservationists might have been seriously injured or killed. Many of the men who participated in hawk shooting in eastern Pennsylvania prior to 1934, and else-where along the Kittatinny Ridge prior to 1956, were rough in-dividuals who had little regard for predators of any kind and less regard for people who wanted them protected. More than once in my own efforts helping Maurice Broun stop the hawk shooting in 1956 at Bake Oven Knob, I was threatened and warned to let the gunners continue their activities. They were not left alone, however, and the killing of migrating hawks as an organized ac-tivity from established shooting blinds on the migration route stopped in 1957, when a new law went into effect in that part of the state. Nevertheless, it was this historic perspective gained in the shooting blinds in 1956, and my reading and discussions with Maurice Broun and others about his efforts years earlier at Hawk Mountain, that gave me an outlook on recreational hawk watching strikingly different from that held by many people who recently joined the ranks of hawkwatchers.

A variety of handout literature also was given to each student, including xerox copies of some of the classic magazine articles that originally called public attention to the hawk slaughter in eastern Pennsylvania and were directly responsible for stimulating action that resulted in the formation of Hawk Mountain Sanctu-ary. These included Richard H. Pough's famous letter "Wholesale Killing of Hawks in Pennsylvania" published in 1932, "Hawk Slaughter at Drehersville" published in 1933 by Henry H. Collins, Jr. in the *Bulletin of the Hawk and Owl Society*, Maurice Broun's classic "Pennsylvania's Bloody Ridges" published in 1956, and others. Thus, students had the opportunity to read the original articles that were part of the foundation of recreational hawk watching today. Other handout literature on falconry and related topics, issued by the Society for the Protection of Birds of Prey (Box 891, Pacific Palisades, California 90272), also was given to each student.

This photograph of dead hawks at Hawk Mountain, taken in 1932, helped to develop support for the establishment of Hawk Mountain Sanctuary. Photo by Richard H. Pough.

The final field trip allowed everybody the opportunity to put to practical use all of the information they learned during the course. Certainly by the time all classroom meetings and field trips were completed, everyone should have developed at least a basic understanding of birds of prey, their flight identification, migration patterns, ecology, man's historic relationship to these predatory birds, and current conservation efforts. Each person should not only have discovered his or her skills, but also weaknesses, as in identification of the rarer or more difficult-to-identify birds. Nevertheless, most people recognized that it was only necessary to spend plenty of days hawk watching in order to become familiar with all the species intimately.

ADDITIONAL READING

Bauer, E. N.
    1982   Winter Roadside Raptor Survey in El Paso County, Colorado, 1962–1979. *Raptor Research*, 16: 10–13.

In 1950 these young conservationists picked up dead hawks shot at Bake Oven Knob, Pennsylvania. Photo by Nelson Hoy.

Broun, M.
  1949 *Hawks Aloft: The Story of Hawk Mountain.* Dodd, Mead Co., New York, N. Y. (Reprinted by Hawk Mountain Sanctuary Assn., Kempton, Pa.)
Brown, L.
  1976a *Birds of Prey: Their Biology and Ecology.* A & W Publishers, New York, N. Y.
  1976b *Eagles of the World.* Universe Books, New York, N. Y.
Craig, T.
  1978 A Car Survey of Raptors in Southeastern Idaho, 1974–76. *Raptor Research*, 12: 40–45.
Enderson, J. H.
  1965 Roadside Raptor Count in Colorado. *Wilson Bulletin*, 77: 82–83.
Gessaman, J. A.
  1982 A Survey of Raptors in Northern Utah, 1976–1979. *Raptor Research*, 16: 4–10.
Grossman, M. L. and J. Hamlet

1964 *Birds of Prey of the World.* Clarkson N. Potter Co., New York, N. Y.

Heintzelman, D. S.
  1975 *Autumn Hawk Flights: The Migrations in Eastern North America.* Rutgers University Press, New Brunswick, N. J.
  1977 A National Inventory of Hawk Migration Lookouts. *Birding*, 9 (2): 57–58.
  1979a *Hawks and Owls of North America.* Universe Books, New York, N. Y.
  1979b *A Guide to Hawk Watching in North America.* Pennsylvania State University Press, University Park, Pa.
  1979c Where Birders Enjoy the Raptor Parade. *Defenders*, 54 (5): 261–264.
  1980 Some Recent Raptor Conservation Efforts in Pennsylvania. *Sierra Club Newsletter* (Pennsylvania Chapter), April 1980 issue, pages 1, 3, & 6.

Johnson, D. L.
  1981 St. Paul's Haven for Broken Birds. *Defenders*, 56 (6):2–7.
  Johnson, D. and J. H. Enderson

  1972 Roadside Raptor Census in Colorado—Winter 1971–72. *Wilson Bulletin*, 84:489–490.

Newton, I.
  1979 *Population Ecology of Raptors.* Buteo Books, Vermillion, S.D.

Potter, J.K.
  1949 Hawks Along the Delaware. *Cassinia*, 37:13–16.

Chapter 7

City Bird Watching

Over the years birdwatchers have developed a tradition of looking for birds in attractive rural, remote, and wilderness areas away from home because splendid birding opportunities frequently are enjoyed in those places. It is the grass-is-greener-on-the-other-side-of-the-fence idea. All too often, however, urban birdwatchers overlook the fine bird-watching opportunities available locally—and even within the borders of some cities. That attitude is very likely to change quickly, however, with the rising cost of gasoline and other transportation. Thus the wise birdwatcher living in an urban setting will want to spend more time birding within the city in which he or she lives—not only to save money on travel but also to get to know better what is to be found close at hand. This chapter, therefore, explores in general terms (with some specific examples) bird-watching opportunities available in many cities and how one may go about exploiting those opportunities easily and quickly. It is a rich field for adventure which far too many birdwatchers have not taken advantage of in years past.

LOONS, GREBES, AND WATERFOWL

Lakes, ponds, streams, and rivers in city parks or elsewhere in urban settings all provide possible bird-watching opportunities for birdwatchers wishing to remain at home, yet wanting to participate in active birding to the fullest extent possible.

Batterson Park Pond in Hartford, Connecticut, for example, provides an example of a city park where fine waterfowl viewing is possible in late autumn. Many birdwatchers in this city look for species such as Ruddy Ducks and Hooded Mergansers in this park.

But excellent waterfowl and other bird-watching areas are not confined only to parks in relatively small cities. Even the largest cities in the world contain excellent birding locations where local birdwatchers gather to enjoy their hobby with gusto after spending long hours among city crowds and congestion.

In New York City, for example, the splendid Jamaica Bay Wildlife Refuge—a unit of Gateway National Recreation Area—embraces some 9,155 acres of open water and tidal marsh within one of the world's largest cities! Because it is located on the Atlantic Flyway, excellent waterfowl and other bird-watching opportunities are available in the refuge. Canada Geese, Brant, Snow Geese, and many species of ducks occur at Jamaica Bay and can be seen without difficulty from a well-maintained gravel path that circles freshwater ponds and passes adjacent to salt marshes. In addition, a nature center and headquarters building provides various natural history exhibits and programs and a staff of professional naturalists welcomes questions and aids visitors in enjoying the refuge's wildlife attractions. As one explores Jamaica Bay Wildlife Refuge, it is sometimes difficult to appreciate that the wildlife that occurs there is within New York City, even though the Manhattan skyline appears nearby. This important refuge provides a vivid example of the importance of refuges in urban areas and the outstanding bird-watching opportunities that can be enjoyed in such places.

In Allentown, Pennsylvania, we also enjoy many fine public parks which contain wetlands suitable for the needs of waterfowl. As a result there are large populations of geese and ducks on these areas, all of which are fair game for the bird-watching enthusiast

The Canada Goose, one of many species of birds observed by birdwatchers at Jamaica Bay Wildlife Refuge in New York City.

active within the urban environment. Late autumn, winter, and spring are the best seasons to enjoy waterfowl watching at these eastern Pennsylvania sites, but even during summer one finds considerable numbers of resident Canada Geese and Mallards with their young on the ponds. Later in the season, however, American Black Ducks, American Wigeon, and a long list of other species also appear. Several local schools and colleges use the parks as teaching resources on their field trips.

Tinicum National Environmental Center in Philadelphia, Pennsylvania, is another outstanding example of a wetland where large numbers of waterfowl and many other species of birds may be seen by millions of city residents. Located within sight and sound of Philadelphia International Airport, birdwatchers nevertheless frequently report a rich variety of species including Canada Geese, Mallards, American Black Ducks, Common Pintails, Green-winged Teal, Blue-winged Teal, American Wigeon, Ruddy Ducks, and

Common Mergansers at Tinicum. Shorebirds and raptors also appear regularly.

On the other hand, Jackson, Mississippi, is a long way from New York City or Philadelphia but its Ross Barnett Reservoir provides birdwatchers in and around Jackson with fine opportunities to see ducks and other waterbirds and the site is used regularly. So, too, is Lake Maggiore Park in St. Petersburg, Florida, where ducks and other waterbirds gather in considerable numbers in winter.

Chicago, Illinois, also has its share of fine birding locations in and near the city. One of these, Grant Park, is well known to Chicago birdwatchers as one of the better places to visit in autumn and winter for seeing ducks and gulls, as well as spring and autumn vireos, warblers, and other songbirds.

Belle Isle in Detroit, Michigan is another excellent example of a fine waterfowl viewing area in winter as large numbers of diving ducks including Redheads, Canvasbacks, Lesser Scaup, Common Goldeneyes, and other species flock off the western and eastern shores of the island. Much productive city waterfowl viewing is, therefore, enjoyed by Detroit birdwatchers at this spot.

In winter, various species of waterfowl including Ring-necked Ducks and Lesser Scaup also are reported in City Park in New Orleans, Louisiana, which makes this location one that birdwatchers in and near this charming southern city frequent in their bird-finding efforts.

Birdwatchers thinking about Arizona may not necessarily think of waterfowl, but there are some fine locations near major urban centers where these birds also can be seen. In Phoenix, for instance, the 300 acres of Encanto Park are visited by birders who look for waterfowl on its wetlands, and in Tucson, Arizona, Reid Park provides an excellent location where a variety of waterbirds are observed. Included are Canvasbacks and other waterfowl.

American White Pelicans are among the waterbird attractions to be enjoyed by birders at Lake Overholser and Lake Hefner in Oklahoma City, Oklahoma. These reservoirs are very attractive for waterbirds from autumn to spring, with the pelicans appearing in April and October.

Countless similar examples of outstanding urban waterfowl viewing sites also exist in other cities across the United States and Canada. In Seattle, Washington, for example, the area along Ubion Bay frequently produces fine autumn and winter waterfowl watching. Birders there look for species such as Gadwall, Blue-winged Teal, Cinnamon Teal, Eurasian Wigeon, Redhead, Barrow's Goldeneye, and Hooded Merganser.

Golden Gate Park in San Francisco, California, provides one final example of an excellent waterfowl and general urban bird-watching area. Stow Lake, one of several within the park, frequently produces Mallards, American Wigeons, Lesser Scaup, and Ruddy Ducks. Elk Glen Lake sometimes produces a Eurasian Wigeon, and Wood Ducks are seen frequently as well. Mallard Lake is especially excellent for feeding ducks, whereas Metson Lake not infrequently produces Wood Ducks. Of course, a great variety of other birds, in addition to waterfowl, also make Golden Gate Park a favored spot for birdwatchers in San Francisco.

HERONS AND EGRETS

Not all cities have habitat suitable for the life-style of herons and egrets, but for birdwatchers living in those urban environments where marshes occur in parks or elsewhere, it is sometimes possible to enjoy fine views of these birds feeding or even nesting. Jamaica Bay Wildlife Refuge in New York City is an outstanding example of an area where various herons and egrets occur and allow easy observation. Another case in point is the shoreside summer resort city of Stone Harbor, New Jersey, which proudly maintains the famous Witmer Stone Bird Sanctuary in which thousands of nesting Common Egrets, Snowy Egrets, Black-crowned Night Herons, and Yellow-crowned Night Herons nest—all within easy view of countless human visitors on the edge of the refuge. Indeed, to large numbers of ordinary people on summer vacation along coastal New Jersey, the heronry at Stone Harbor is one of the natural history highlights of the area and a place where one may see and study (not infrequently for the first time) these birds at will for as long or short a period as they wish. For birdwatchers the heronry is even more important—a marvelous example of an urban habitat where some of our most spectacular herons and egrets occur.

HAWKS

Hawk watchers normally think of hawk lookouts or locations where diurnal birds of prey can be observed during migration or in other concentrations as being located in rural or wilderness areas, and famous sites such as Bake Oven Knob and Hawk Mountain Sanctuary in eastern Pennsylvania are located in such places. In point of fact, however, it sometimes is possible to use the tops of roofs or backyards as hawk lookouts in many cities in the United States (particularly the East) and Canada. One city fireman I know often sits outside the firehouse to which he is assigned in Allentown, Pennsylvania, and looks for migrating Broad-winged Hawks or other species passing overhead. While he does not see the large numbers of birds that are seen at nearby important hawk lookouts in the area, he nevertheless sees some migrating hawks as a reward for his efforts. Thus, if one can't leave the urban environment for one reason or another, it still may be possible to observe migrating hawks simply by sitting on the top of a roof, in a backyard, or on some city hilltop looking for passing raptors.

On the other hand, there are several superb hawk migration lookouts located within or very close to large cities in the United States and Canada, and it is worthwhile to discuss a few of these to illustrate the superb hawk-watching opportunities that are possible in some cities. One such lookout, an excellent spring site, is Braddock Bay State Park near Rochester, New York, as demonstrated nicely by the splendid efforts of Laura Moon and others of the Genesee Ornithological Society of Rochester. Tens of thousands of migrating Broad-winged Hawks, Sharp-shinned Hawks, and numerous other species pass this site in spring. Birdwatchers from all around the Rochester area stop at Braddock Bay to enjoy hawk watching and discussions of other bird-watching events and opportunities.

Equally exciting are two autumn hawk lookouts known to all experienced hawk watchers in North America—both sites within cities. Over the years countless thousands of hawk watchers have visited the Montclair Hawk Lookout Sanctuary overlooking Montclair, New Jersey, where the Montclair Bird Club maintains an annual autumn hawk count. Under the skilled direction of pioneer hawk watcher Andrew Bihun, Jr., who serves as the hawk count coordinator, this site has produced some of the memorable hawk flights reported in the past in the East. At times more than 10,000 migrating Broad-winged Hawks have been counted from the top of the old quarry which forms the lookout—all within sight of New York City and its millions of citizens. Farther west, at the southwestern tip of Lake Superior, the Hawk Ridge Nature Reserve provides some of the very finest autumn hawk watching anywhere in the Great Lakes region within the city of Duluth. Like Montclair in New Jersey, Hawk Ridge is an urban lookout with a distinctive wild flavor and plenty of birdlife to reward even the most fanatical hawk watchers!

It is clear, therefore, that no birdwatcher should give up in frustration if he or she can't race to a wilderness hawk lookout on a day that seemingly looks favorable for a good flight of hawks. There are many sites, perhaps minor when compared with major lookouts of known significance, that nevertheless can be used for

Hawk watchers on the lookout at Hawk Ridge Nature Reserve, Duluth, Minnesota.

a few hours of urban hawk watching when one's time is limited and it is necessary to remain near home in the city. Far too many city birdwatchers don't look up to see what may be passing overhead!

SHOREBIRDS

Most birdwatchers don't consider the possibilities of watching shorebirds within the confines of cities, yet at some such locations good shorebirding opportunities exist. For example, lake beds that are drained for one reason or another often attract a varied assortment of sandpipers, plovers, yellowlegs, and other species during July and August. Similarly, at mud and silt flats along rivers, creeks, and elsewhere in wetlands within cities one sometimes finds shorebirds as well. It simply is necessary to seek them carefully. For example, the mud and silt flats in the Tinicum National Environmental Center in Philadelphia, Pennsylvania, often produce fine assortments of shorebirds. So, too, does the famous Jamaica Bay Wildlife Refuge in New York City where hundreds of migrating shorebirds, including White-rumped Sandpipers, rest and feed within the refuge.

Not infrequently, however, it is manmade habitats that are most attractive to shorebirds and thus offer the best bird-watching opportunities for shorebird buffs. For example, the sewage lagoons at the Trenton, New Jersey, sewage treatment plant provide fine shorebirding during July and August, as witnessed by the repeated observation of Killdeer, Lesser Yellowlegs, and various sandpipers—Spotted, Solitary, Pectoral, Least, and Semi-palmated. Occasionally other species also appear as isolated individuals.

Relatively little is known about the use of sewage lagoons by shorebirds, but from the information available it appears that the attraction for the birds is a rich, concentrated food supply. In addition, unlike tidal mudflats which are subject to periodic flooding, the sewage lagoons provide a continuously available feeding and resting site. Thus it is likely that similar facilities in other cities also will provide good shorebird-watching opportunities and thus should be examined repeatedly and carefully for these birds.

GULLS

Along the harbors, and other wetlands, of many cities on the Atlantic and Pacific coasts of North America (as well as some inland sites), a variety of species of gulls occur—often in considerable numbers. For example, birdwatchers working the Portland, Maine, harbor in winter make a special effort to look for Glaucous, Iceland, and Bonaparte's Gulls whereas the harbors around New York City produce Herring and Ring-billed Gulls at all seasons. And, during April and May, New York City birders look for Bonaparte's Gulls and the rare Little Gull. Farther inland, at Buffalo, New York, winter gull watching can produce a rich variety of species such as Greater Black-backed, Herring, Ring-billed, Glaucous, and Iceland Gulls. More rarely, during migration, Little, Franklin's, Black-headed, and Sabine's Gulls also are seen occasionally.

OWLS

The possibility of seeing or hearing owls in cities is excellent in many sections of North America, as many birdwatchers have discovered. Generally common and widely distributed species such as Screech Owls are most likely to be found in parks and other wooded areas, especially when rivers, creeks, streams, or other wetlands are present. At other times, as in Lubbock, Texas, in Mackenzie State Park, a colony of Burrowing Owls is easily seen living among a prairie dog town. Winter, too, often is a good time to seek owls in some cities such as Duluth, Minnesota, where Snowy, Great Gray, and Boreal Owls sometimes are reported. Not infrequently, owls are more common within cities than many birdwatchers realize simply because they did not take the time and make the effort to look for them.

NIGHTHAWKS AND SWIFTS

Pick any summer evening in the United States and the urban birdwatcher should have no difficulty in seeing Common Nighthawks flying overhead while uttering their loud, nasal *peent* at frequent intervals. It is a common crepuscular species in many

A Herring Gull.

North American cities and one familiar to most birders. So, too, is the Chimney Swift in the eastern United States, where it often is seen swooping over city skies along with the larger nighthawks. West of the Rockies, however, one looks for Vaux's Swifts in place of eastern Chimney Swifts. Thus both nighthawks and swifts, of one species of another, are birds one comes to expect to see in an urban sky. They are good birds to show to beginners and children, who may not know much about birds but might be eager to learn. The fact that these species are easily observed, and readily identified, makes them excellent subjects to demonstrate to such persons.

HUMMINGBIRDS

One may not normally think of a city as a place to see hummingbirds, but where reasonably large gardens exist, it is certainly

Nestling Barn Owls sometimes are discovered in old buildings in cities. Photo by Allan D. Cruickshank.

possible to observe and enjoy hummingbirds within the urban environment. In the East, the Ruby-throated Hummingbird is the species to look for, whereas in the western cities one might encounter a variety of species best identified by reference to one of the standard guides to bird identification. In Los Angeles, California, for example, one of the best locations for finding a variety of species of hummingbirds is in the South Coast Botanic Gardens where Anna's, Costa's, Allen's, and sometimes Rufous and Calliope Hummingbirds are reported.

Regardless of species, however, if one is fortunate in having hummingbirds visiting a garden, it is worthwhile to place hummingbird feeders—filled with red sugar water—in various spots for use by the birds which consume enormous quantities each day. Thus these unique New World birds can add great charm and interest to any city backyard garden in which they might happen to appear.

WOODPECKERS

Any city birdwatcher with an active bird feeding program almost certainly will have a few woodpeckers visiting suet feeders. Among the species likely to be seen within the urban setting, such as my home in Allentown, Pennsylvania, are Common Flickers, Hairy Woodpeckers, and Downy Woodpeckers. It is widely distributed species as these that urban birdwatchers come to know in their backyard feeding stations, but occasionally other rarer species also appear to add delight to one's observation efforts. In fact, the possibility of seeing one of the other rarer species in an urban setting adds spice to city bird watching. Thus a three-toed woodpecker or a Pileated Woodpecker might appear unexpectedly for a few hours or days despite the fact that neither species is to be expected in such settings.

A Ruby-throated Hummingbird at a garden feeder.

WOOD WARBLERS

Although wood warblers normally are very restricted in numbers of species breeding in urban settings, most city parks of any size with adequate habitat support a few species of warblers such as Black-and-whites, Yellowthroats, or Ovenbirds (in the East). During the spring and autumn migrations, however, just about any species of warbler known to occur with regularity in a given state might appear in the urban park setting. Thus warbler buffs generally have no difficulty finding their fascinating subjects at those times of the year. Even the largest cities such as New York produce excellent warbler-watching opportunities in Central Park and elsewhere in spring and autumn. It simply is a matter of going to these places and looking for the birds early in the morning. Much the same also can be said for finding vireos in similar situations, not infrequently mixed among flocks of migrating warblers.

Birdwatchers living in, or near, Allentown, Pennsylvania, for example, find Robin Hood Woods in Lehigh Parkway and Waldheim Park on South Mountain both excellent locations for finding migrating wood warblers, vireos, and many other woodland species during the spring and autumn migration seasons. Hybrid wood warblers as rare as the elusive Lawrence's Warbler have even nested in Waldheim Park, and the South Mountain range is one of the rare locations in Lehigh County where the Veery is a nesting species.

In Wilmington, Delaware, birdwatchers find Alapocos Woods—a 109 acre park—a fine location in spring for finding various species of vireos, wood warblers, thrushes, and other songbirds.

And so it is in many other sections of the country. In Little Rock, Arkansas, for instance, Boyle Park provides birders with fine opportunities to see many migrating birds including vireos and wood warblers, plus a good many other types of birds during the spring migration. Moreover, after the spring migration is completed and the nesting season begins, a good many species of wood warblers and other woodland birds nest there, including such fine species as Prothonotary, Yellow-throated, and Kentucky Warblers. Wood warblers always are delightful to observe, regardless of where they are encountered.

FINCHES AND SPARROWS

Because of the great popularity of backyard bird feeding, urban birdwatchers have many fine opportunities to observe a variety of finches and sparrows at such feeding stations within the confines of cities. Cardinals, grosbeaks, finches, goldfinches, towhees, and various sparrows all eagerly flock at feeding stations in winter to obtain food. Thus at least the more common species of finches and sparrows likely to occur in a particular area are usually readily observed at city bird feeding stations. And, adding adventure to the activity, is the real possibility that some rarer species might also appear as well.

ZOO BIRD WATCHING

Most large cities have zoological parks with collections of birds from various parts of the world. Among the notable examples are the Bronx Zoo in New York City, the Philadelphia Zoo, and the San Diego Zoo. At the Bronx Zoo, for instance, the city birdwatcher has splendid opportunities to observe not only native North American species but many fascinating birds from the American tropics—all set in life-like tropical forest settings. For those interested in waterfowl, the Philadelphia Zoo has an exceptional collection of these birds from around the world, and the natural settings of the famous San Diego Zoo also offer much fine recreational bird watching.

While birdwatchers generally would not include zoo birds on their lists of species observed, visits to zoos provide birdwatchers with excellent opportunities to see many species alive and develop identification skills via the use of captive birds. Then, when vacations or other trips are made to those parts of the world where the zoo birds occur in the wild, the birdwatcher already has some experience with the birds.

NATURAL HISTORY MUSEUMS

Birdwatchers living in large cities in the United States and Canada generally have available to them the facilities of excellent

The flamingo pond at Sea World in San Diego, California. Photo by Sea World.

natural history museums, although many birders are not aware of how valuable and useful visits to such institutions can be.

To begin, most natural history museums (exceptions are certain research institutions) have excellent exhibits and displays of native and foreign birds—often in natural habitat groups or dioramas. Every birdwatcher can benefit from visits to such exhibits and study of the species on display. However, beginning and intermediate level birders will find such use of natural history museum bird exhibits especially valuable as an educational aid in learning to identify correctly both common and rarer native birds.

More advanced birdwatchers will also find the extensive scientific research collections of study skins of birds a priceless research and teaching tool. In large museums, very large series of specimens of species and subspecies are available for study to qualified persons including serious amateur birdwatchers. Only by handling and studying such large series of museum specimens can birdwatchers develop an adequate awareness and apprecia-

A Bronze-winged Duck in a zoo. Birdwatchers can see many exotic birds in zoos and become familiar with them.

tion of the variation in size and pattern of plumage that many species exhibit—and which most birdwatchers are unaware of, if they restrict their bird-watching activities only to field observation of birds. Certainly, it does not take birdwatchers with experience working with museum research collections long to realize that all field guides illustrate only typical plumages of birds while necessarily ignoring less common variations. That is one reason why some birds observed in the field do not match illustrations in a field guide exactly.

Large natural history museums also have another vital birdwatcher's resource of great value to advanced birders—especially if they are engaged in research projects. That is the museum's library of ornithological books and journals. Often it is necessary to consult the published literature about a particular bird topic, and it is then that the library holdings of large natural history museums are of enormous value to city birdwatchers. Most publications that are needed are included in such collections.

Finally, most large natural history museums have ornithology departments in which professional ornithologists are employed. Some of these people will agree to answer reasonable questions about birds either on the telephone or when birdwatchers visit their offices and laboratories. However, such behind-the-scenes visits to museum bird departments should be made by appointment only, since the scientists working in museums are busily engaged in important research and do not always have time to meet every demand from the public without prior notice. Some natural history museums also have education departments which may be able to answer some questions.

There are many hundreds of museums and other institutions that house bird collections of one sort or another, but a survey in 1973 by the American Ornithologists' Union of such bird collections in the United States and Canada showed that only a small number were major in size and importance. The twenty largest bird collections in museums and other institutions are listed here along with the number of study skins in their holdings.

American Museum of Natural History, New York City	900,000
National Museum of Natural History, Washington, D. C.	400,000
Field Museum of Natural History, Chicago, Ill.	300,000
Museum of Comparative Zoology, Cambridge, Mass.	300,000
University of Michigan, Ann Arbor, Mich.	200,000
Academy of Natural Sciences, Philadelphia, Pa.	160,000
Carnegie Museum of Natural History, Pittsburgh, Pa.	150,000
Museum of Vertebrate Zoology, Berkeley, Ca.	150,000
Royal Ontario Museum, Toronto, Ontario	105,000
Los Angeles County Museum, Los Angeles, Ca.	90,000
California Academy of Sciences, San Francisco, Ca.	84,000
Peabody Museum, Yale University, New Haven, Conn.	80,000
Moore Laboratory of Zoology, Los Angeles, Ca.	67,000
Louisiana State University, Baton Rouge, La.	65,000
National Museum of Canada, Ottawa, Ontario	58,000
University of Kansas, Lawrence, Kan.	40,000
San Diego Natural History Museum, San Diego, Ca.	37,000
University of California, Los Angeles, Ca.	36,500
Denver Museum of Natural History, Denver, Colo.	35,000
Cornell University, Ithaca, N. Y.	34,200

Birdwatchers needing a more comprehensive listing of natural history museums and other institutions containing bird collections should refer to the report by Richard C. Banks, Mary H. Clench, and Jon C. Barlow entitled "Bird Collections in the United States and Canada" published in *The Auk* (1973: 136–170). There are numerous smaller collections in many sections of the United States and Canada that might serve the needs of birdwatchers included in this detailed listing.

ADDITIONAL READING

Harrison, G. H.
  1979 *The Backyard Bird Watcher*. Simon and Schuster, New York, N. Y.
Heintzelman, D. S.
  1978 *North American Ducks, Geese & Swans*. Winchester Press, New York, N. Y.
  1979a *A Guide to Hawk Watching in North America*. Pennsylvania State University Press, University Park, Pa.
  1979b *Hawks and Owls of North America*. Universe Books, New York, N. Y.
Leck, C. F. and P. Hawkins
  1979 Observations of Shorebirds at Selected New Jersey Sewage Lagoons. *Cassinia*, 57: 3–5.
Murphy, D.
  1980 Birding Golden Gate Park. *Birding,* 12 (5): 158–164.
Pettingill, O. S. Jr.
  1977 *A Guide to Bird Finding East of the Mississippi*. Second Edition. Oxford University Press, New York, N. Y.
  1981 *A Guide to Bird Finding West of the Mississippi*. Second Edition. Oxford University Press, New York, N. Y.
Webster, G.
  1980 City Birding. *Bird Watcher's Digest,* 2 (4): 80–85..

Chapter 8

Experimental Bird Feeding

Within recent years millions of people in the United States and Canada have established backyard bird feeders during winter in an effort to supply a variety of wild birds with adequate supplies of food to assure winter survival of these wildlife resources. In large measure, the biological and ecological impact of winter backyard bird feeding is not really known. In the fourth edition of *A Field Guide to the Birds,* however, Roger Tory Peterson suggests that the increased interest in birds and winter feeding resulting from use of his field guides may have helped to produce geographic range expansions of some species such as Mourning Doves, Tufted Titmice, Northern Cardinals, Evening Grosbeaks, and perhaps some other species.

It is curious, therefore, in spite of the enormous public interest in winter bird feeding, that very little research has been conducted to determine the best types of foods to be fed to specific species of birds visiting backyard bird feeders. Generally mixtures of various seeds are sold as wild birdseed based upon the opinions of the people preparing the mixtures, rather than data secured during field trials in various sections of the United States and Canada.

Here, then, are excellent and enjoyable opportunities to experiment with various types of birdseeds to determine which are most preferred by specific species of wild birds in different geographic areas of North America. Not only will wild birds benefit from our having more accurate knowledge of their food preferences, but the cost of operating winter bird feeders might be reduced in some instances.

Fortunately for people interested in starting experimental bird feeding projects, a few such pioneering studies are available to serve as models upon which similar experimental projects can be patterned. Especially important are *The Backyard Bird Watcher* by George H. Harrison and "Relative Attractiveness of Different Foods at Wild Bird Feeders" by Aelred D. Geis. It is worthwhile, therefore, to look at some of the results of these two studies.

According to George Harrison, the following seeds were poor or useless as food for use in wild bird feeders: wheat, milo, red millet, hulled whole oats (oat groats), broken white rice, sterilized hemp, and buckwheat. On the other hand, the following seeds were good to excellent foods for use at winter bird feeders: gray-striped sunflower seeds, black-striped sunflower seeds, white mil-

Evening Grosbeaks at a bird feeder.

let, peanut hearts, crushed hulled oats mixed with peanut hearts, fine cracked yellow corn, canary seed (Argentine and Moroccan), Niger seed, and dwarf or yellow millet.

More detailed in its results and conclusions is the Aelred Geis study conducted in Maryland for the United States Fish and Wildlife Service. It reported: "Many common bird foods, such as fine cracked corn, wheat, sorghum, hulled oats, and rice, were found to be relatively unattractive. Seeds of the small black oil-type sunflower were superior to those of black-striped and gray-striped sunflowers. White proso millet was the best seed for use in attracting the small seed-eating species. Feeding preferences among various species of birds are strikingly different; consequently it is difficult to formulate a mixture of seeds that would be efficient at all locations and at all times." The following table, however, provides a summary of various species of birds and the seeds they preferred in winter in Maryland.

Species	*Seeds preferred*
American Goldfinch	Hulled sunflower seeds (pieces or whole kernels), thistle seed, oil-type sunflower seeds
Blue Jay	Whole peanut kernels, black-striped sunflower seeds, gray-striped sunflower seeds
Brown-headed Cowbird	White proso millet
Northern Cardinal	Oil-type sunflower seeds
Carolina Chickadee	Oil-type sunflower seeds
Dark-eyed Junco	Red proso millet, white proso millet
Common Grackle	Hulled sunflower seeds, cracked corn
Evening Grosbeak	Oil-type sunflower seeds
House Finch	Oil-type sunflower seeds
House Sparrow	White proso millet
Mourning Dove	Small black oil-type sunflower seeds
Purple Finch	Oil-type sunflower seeds
Red-bellied Woodpecker	Black-striped sunflower seeds, cracked corn
Song Sparrow	White proso millet
Starling	Peanut hearts, hulled oats

Tree Sparrow	Red proso millet, white proso millet
Tufted Titmouse	Peanut kernels
White-crowned Sparrow	Oil-type sunflower seeds, white proso millet
White-throated Sparrow	Oil-type sunflower seeds, white proso millet, black-striped sunflower seeds

Among the general conclusions reported in the Geis study are that consumption usually was proportional to relative seed attractiveness, peanut kernels were eaten at a considerably greater rate than would be suggested by the number of feeder visits, and thistle seed allowed for over twice the number of visits that one would have expected. Thistle seed, therefore, was considered a relatively efficient food. By far the oil-type sunflower seeds and white proso millet were the best winter bird feeder foods used under Maryland ecological conditions. Certainly one might wish to supplement commercial or other mixtures of bird seed with these two excellent bird foods.

In addition to the two previously described experimental bird feeding studies, Emily Grey also made a detailed field study of types of seeds that some eighteen bird species preferred at Blacksburg, Virginia, during the period December 1975 through March 1976. Some species preferred specific types of food, but not all species liked the same types of seeds. Results and conclusions of Grey's study are summarized here.

Mourning Doves much preferred proso millet although corn-proso millet-sunflower seeds, wheat-proso millet-hegari milo, and commercial Kroger mixtures also were consumed.

Blue Jays tended to prefer seeds such as sunflowers, whole peanuts and, to a lesser degree, corn.

Chickadees and Tufted Titmice liked sunflower seeds and whole peanuts best, but hardly touched mixes of birdseeds.

European Starlings, not a native North American species, selected peanut hearts, then oat groats. A variety of other items also were consumed.

House Sparrows, another introduced species, liked proso millet best, but German millet also was consumed to a considerable degree.

Northern Cardinals, which always add color and charm to a bird feeding station, by far preferred sunflower seeds, then a combination of milo and hegari milo.

Evening Grosbeaks, which Maurice Broun at Hawk Mountain called "Grospigs" because they ate tons of sunflower seeds at the refuge, not unexpectedly preferred sunflower seeds.

Purple Finches also liked sunflower seeds as their top-of-the-line menu item.

White-crowned Sparrows tended to select a considerable variety of items in the assortment offered. Included were German millet, pearl millet, proso millet, browntop millet, oat groats, and hegari milo.

White-throated Sparrows also selected a great variety of items. Included were sunflower seeds, proso millet, German millet, pearl millet, whole peanuts, combine milo, corn, brown top millet, and rice.

Song Sparrows, on the other hand, only had two particularly desirable foods—proso millet and German millet.

It is clear from these studies that birds that typically visit bird feeders eat a varied assortment of seeds and other items, but which items are consumed depends upon which birds are at the feeders. The best way to determine which seeds are most attractive to birds in a particular geographic area of North America is to conduct one's own feeder food experiment, then buy the preferred items at feed mills or other agricultural stores and mix your own birdseed combinations.

Birdwatchers wishing to conduct experimental bird feeding studies should, first of all, keep their experiments simple and relatively limited. One can, for example, build a simple feeding tray, divided into five or six sections, into which a different type of seed or other food is placed. Then it is a matter of watching and counting the number of visits to each type of food made by each species. After a few months of this type of investigation, enough information should be available to develop a reasonably good idea of the food preferences of the various species of birds visiting a feeding station. The mixture that one prepares, therefore, can be adjusted to the desires of the local bird population and the emphasis one wishes to place on attracting particular bird species to a feeding station.

ADDITIONAL READING

Dennis, J. V.
  1978   *A Complete Guide to Bird Feeding.* Alfred A. Knopf, New York, N. Y.

Geis, A. D.
  1980   *Relative Attractiveness of Different Foods at Wild Bird Feeders.* U. S. Fish and Wildlife Service Special Scientific Report—Wildlife No. 233, Washington, D. C.

Grey, E.
  1978   A Budgeted Banquet for the Birds. *Birding,* 10 (6): 323–326.

Harrison, G. H.
  1979   *The Backyard Bird Watcher.* Simon and Schuster, New York, N. Y.

Peterson, R. T.
  1980   *A Field Guide to the Birds.* Fourth Edition. Houghton Mifflin Co., Boston, Mass.

Chapter 9

Collecting Bird-Related Items

The primary objective of bird watching is to observe and enjoy wild birds in their natural habitats, but many birders also are eager collectors of a wide variety of bird-related items. Indeed, some birders develop avid second hobbies by collecting bird stamps, duck and other decoys, wildlife art, and other items. The list is almost endless. This chapter, however, examines some of the more popular bird-related collectibles and thus provides a primer on the subject.

BIRD STAMPS

Collecting stamps featuring pictures of birds is one of the many activities that some birdwatchers enjoy when they can't be outside watching live birds. There are various aspects of this activity, part of a branch of topical stamp collecting termed biophilately, but which might better be termed avianphilately. Some people, for example, collect postage stamps featuring bird portraits. Other

persons collect federal duck stamps issued annually by the United
States Department of the Interior. Still others collect duck stamps
issued by various states and private organizations, turkey stamps
issued by the National Wild Turkey Federation, state habitat stamps,
and/or wildlife conservation stamps issued by the National Wildlife Federation.

By combining each of these types of avianphilately, one has
more than abundant opportunity to spend countless pleasant, educational hours indoors relaxing with bird-related items.

Postage Stamps

Prior to the spring of 1982, birdwatchers interested in collecting
United States postage stamps featuring wild birds had far fewer
issues to add to a collection than were available from various
foreign countries. Indeed, since the first such stamp was issued
on December 6, 1967—the Everglades National Park stamp showing an egret—only a dozen issues (some with several stamps per
issue) had appeared through early 1980. That situation was changed
dramatically, however, in the spring of 1982 when the United
States Postal Service issued its strikingly beautiful birds and flowers of the states collection featuring the state bird and state flower
of each of our fifty states. The celebrated bird artist Arthur Singer
painted the portraits of the birds, and his son Alan Singer painted
the flower portraits—the first known father and son team to design
and paint a United States postage stamp issue. Full technical
details on United States postage stamps are available in the *Scott
Specialized Catalogue of United States Stamps*.

Canadian postage stamps featuring pictures of birds also are of
interest to many birdwatcher-stamp collectors. Canada, however,
has only a limited number of stamps featuring birds. Nevertheless,
one in particular—the Peregrine Falcon stamp issued in 1978—
is especially attractive.

As one becomes involved in collecting bird postage stamps, it
is possible to concentrate on only selected groups of birds such
as diurnal birds of prey. To do so requires collecting stamps issued
by numerous foreign countries, as well as the United States. Po-
land, for example, issued several raptor stamps, as have several
other foreign countries. Much of the same requirements apply as

A United States postage stamp featuring one of America's many species of birds.

one develops collections of bird stamps devoted to other groups of birds—perhaps seabirds, waterfowl, or songbirds.

Regardless of which bird stamps one collects, the birdwatcher-stamp collector will find *Birds of the World on Stamps,* published by the American Topical Association, an essential reference. It not only lists, by families and species, all of the postage stamps of the world featuring birds, but these same stamps also are listed by the name of the country which issued them. Thus one can approach the subject from either way and determine easily and accurately the number of stamps to be collected and the species of birds depicted on the stamps.

As one becomes more than mildly interested in collecting postage stamps featuring pictures of birds, it is helpful to join the American Topical Association, 3306 North 50th St., Milwaukee, Wisconsin 53216, and receive its publication *Topical Times.* Also available from the organization are various topical handbooks, such as *Birds of the World on Stamps.* The biology unit of the ATA also issues its own periodical, *Bio-Philately,* at modest additional cost.

To begin collecting postage stamps, however, birdwatchers may wish to purchase a "Birds and Butterflies Stamp Collecting Kit" for a few dollars from the United States Postal Service. The kit is readily available at most post offices.

Federal Duck Stamps

Perhaps the most popular stamps depicting birds are not postage stamps but rather Migratory Bird Hunting and Conservation Stamps—popularly known as federal duck stamps—issued each year, since 1934, by the United States Department of the Interior. All persons, sixteen years of age or older, wishing to hunt migratory waterfowl in the United States must purchase and sign a federal duck stamp, in addition to a state hunting license. However, many nonhunters, including a good many birdwatchers, also buy federal duck stamps because they help to save wildlife habitat and make excellent stamps to collect.

The purpose of the sale of federal duck stamps is to raise money to purchase refuge and propagation habitat for the conservation of waterfowl and other migratory birds. Over the years the program has been extraordinarily successful in meeting its goal. Indeed, from 1934 to June 30, 1976, in excess of $176 million was raised through duck stamp sales! That money was used to acquire well over one million acres of land used for waterfowl and wildlife refuges and waterfowl production areas.

Federal duck stamps may be purchased from all first and second class post offices, from the Philatelic Sales Agency of the U. S. Postal Service, and from certain other sources. The earliest issues, prior to 1941, are rare, expensive, and available only through stamp dealers and private individuals because all unsold duck stamps issued prior to 1941 were destroyed after the year of issue expired. However, most of the issues are available at premium prices from many sources including stamp dealers and sources with ads appearing in *Ducks Unlimited* magazine.

The following table summarizes some of the basic information about each of the federal duck stamps issued.

Year	Species Shown	Artist
1934–35	Mallards	Jay N. "Ding" Darling

The 1978–79 Migratory Bird Hunting and Conservation Stamp, popularly known as a duck stamp, featuring a Hooded Merganser painted by wildlife artist Albert Earl Gilbert.

Year	Species Shown	Artist
1935–36	Canvasbacks	Frank W. Benson
1936–37	Canada Geese	Richard E. Bishop
1937–38	Greater Scaup	J. D. Knap
1938–39	Common Pintails	Roland Clark
1939–40	Green-winged Teal	Lynn Bogue Hunt
1940–41	American Black Ducks	Francis Lee Jaques
1941–42	Ruddy Ducks	E. R. Kalmbach
1942–43	American Wigeons	A. Lassel Ripley
1943–44	Wood Ducks	Walter E. Bohl
1944–45	White-fronted Geese	Walter A. Weber
1945–46	Northern Shovelers	Owen J. Gromme
1946–47	Redheads	Bob Hines
1947–48	Snow Geese	Jack Murray
1948–49	Buffleheads	Maynard Reece
1949–50	Common Goldeneyes	"Roge" E. Preuss
1950–51	Trumpeter Swans	Walter A. Weber

The 1979–80 federal duck stamp featuring Green-winged Teals painted by Kenneth L. Michaelsen.

Year	Species Shown	Artist
1951–52	Gadwalls	Maynard Reece
1952–53	Harlequin Ducks	John H. Dick
1953–54	Blue-winged Teal	Clayton B. Seagears
1954–55	Ring-necked Ducks	Harvey D. Sandstrom
1955–56	Blue Geese	Stanley Stearns
1956–57	American Mergansers	Edward J. Bierly
1957–58	Common Eiders	Jackson Miles Abbott
1958–59	Canada Geese	Leslie C. Kouba
1959–60	Labrador Retriever with Mallard	Maynard Reece
1960–61	Redheads	John A. Ruthven
1961–62	Mallards	Edward A. Morris
1962–63	Common Pintails	Edward A. Morris
1963–64	Brant	Edward J. Bierly
1964–65	Nene (Hawaiian Geese)	Stanley Stearns
1965–66	Canvasbacks	Ron Jenkins
1966–67	Whistling Swans	Stanley Stearns

Year	Species Shown	Artist
1967–68	Oldsquaws	Leslie C. Kouba
1968–69	Hooded Mergansers	C. G. Pritchard
1969–70	White-winged Scoters	Maynard Reece
1970–71	Ross' Geese	Edward J. Bierly
1971–72	Cinnamon Teal	Maynard Reece
1972–73	Emperor Geese	Arthur M. Cook
1973–74	Steller's Eiders	Lee LeBlanc
1974–75	Wood Ducks	David A. Maass
1975–76	Canvasback decoy	James L. Fisher
1976–77	Canada Geese	Anderson Magee
1977–78	Ross' Geese	Martin R. Murk
1978–79	Hooded Merganser	Albert Earl Gilbert
1979–80	Green-winged Teal	Kenneth L. Michaelsen
1980–81	Mallards	Richard W. Plasschaert
1981–82	Ruddy Ducks	John S. Wilson
1982–83	Canvasbacks	David A. Maass

State Duck Stamps

Within recent years a growing number of states have issued and sold their own annual versions of duck stamps to raise additional money for waterfowl conservation. California, in 1971, was the first state to issue a state duck stamp. In 1972, Iowa issued its first duck stamp followed by Maryland in 1974. Since then many states have joined the effort and doubtless more will follow in the future. The following table summarizes the current status of state duck stamp issues.

State	Year First Stamp was Issued
Alabama	1979
Arkansas	1981
California	1971
Delaware	1980
Florida	1979
Illinois	1975
Indiana	1976
Iowa	1972
Maryland	1974
Massachusetts	1975

Wood Ducks, painted by Walter Wolfe, used on the 1979–80 California duck stamp. Photo by California Department of Fish and Game.

State	Year First Stamp was Issued
Michigan	1976
Minnesota	1977
Mississippi	1976
Missouri	1979
Montana	1978
Nebraska	1979
Nevada	1979
North Dakota	1982
Ohio	1982
Oklahoma	1980
South Carolina	1981
South Dakota	1976
Tennessee	1979
Texas	1981
Wisconsin	1978

With the availability of state duck stamps, the stamp collector has added material to place in a collection of bird stamps. Such stamps can either be purchased at full issue value upon availability or after they have expired at a greatly reduced rate in some instances. Thus California, for example, issues its expired duck stamps at the rate of one dollar per sheet of five stamps for those years for which stamps are available still. This provides collectors with ample opportunity to obtain the stamps for some years after a given issue has appeared.

Long Island Duck Stamp

Each year since 1977, a Long Island duck stamp has been issued by the Long Island Wetlands and Waterfowl League, Inc. (P. O. Box 84, Babylon, N. Y. 11702) to help support the cause of wetland and waterfowl conservation. The paintings from which the stamps are printed also are reproduced as limited edition prints with copies, including some that are remarqued, also available from the League. Thus stamp and wildlife art print collectors also can add these regional offerings to their collections. In 1977 American Black Ducks painted by Peter Corbin appeared on the stamp; in 1978 Hooded Mergansers by Robert Hettinger, Jr. were used; and in 1979 Common Goldeneyes by Diane Pierce were featured on the stamp.

Wild Turkey Stamps

Since 1976, the National Wild Turkey Federation—a non-profit, private education, conservation, and research organization dedicated to research and conservation of Wild Turkeys—has issued an annual Wild Turkey stamp. These are attractive and patterned after the federal duck stamps but, of course, are *not* required to be purchased by turkey hunters. Nevertheless, many Wild Turkey hunters—and some birdwatchers—buy a turkey stamp anyway to support the work of the Federation and as a speculative investment. As with many federal duck stamps, which have increased markedly in value, they hope the value of the turkey stamps also will increase in the future. Other buyers do so simply because they enjoy collecting the stamps as attractive issues.

The 1979 Long Island Wetlands and Waterfowl League, Inc., duck stamp featuring Common Goldeneyes painted by Dianee Pierce.

In 1979, the Federation also issued the first of five annual Wild Turkey Research Stamps, as a second type of issue. The money received from the sale of this stamp will be applied to the construction of a unique Wild Turkey Research Center to be located in Edgefield, South Carolina.

A history of this organization's efforts is contained in *A Catalog of the Wild Turkey Stamp Prints with Biographies of the Artists* by Russell A. Fink. Copies of this book-stamp album are available from the National Wild Turkey Federation, P. O. Box 467, Edgefield, S. C. 29824.

NATIONAL WILDLIFE FEDERATION STAMPS

Since 1938, the National Wildlife Federation has issued each year sheets of wildlife conservation stamps the sale of which provides a considerable portion of the funds the Federation uses to pay for its varied programs. Jay "Ding" Darling designed and

The 1979 Wild Turkey stamp issuued by the National Wild Turkey Federation. The birds were painted by Ken Carlson.

painted the pictures used on the first set of stamps and, over the years, most well-known wildlife artists of America have had some of their paintings featured on the stamps.

During the years that the stamps have been issued, dozens of species of birds have been featured to the delight of birdwatchers, conservationists, and stamp collectors. The Northern Cardinal remains the most popular of the species shown to date because of its beautiful red plumage.

Recently a new tool—a complete index to forty-three years of stamp subjects, with each species and the year(s) it appeared— was issued by the Federation. This index makes it possible to accurately and quickly determine when a particular species appeared on a stamp. Attractive, inexpensive albums also are available for persons wishing to preserve the stamps in an organized manner, and back issues of many stamps can be purchased from the National Wildlife Federation, 1412 16th St., N. W., Washington, D. C. 20036. Collecting these attractive wildlife stamps,

The 1979 Wild Turkey research stamp issued by the National Wild Turkey Federation.

therefore, is one important aspect of collecting wildlife-related objects for birdwatchers.

RAPTOR FUND STAMPS

In 1981 the Raptor Fund, Inc. (P. O. Box 704, Oak Park, Illinois 60303) issued a raptor stamp, using a painting by Richard Sloan of a Peregrine Falcon in flight, and a limited edition art print of the same painting. In 1982, a stamp and print made from a painting of a Bald Eagle by Ned Smith was issued.

The purpose of selling these stamps and prints is to raise funds to support various raptor conservation programs. These include providing financial support for captive breeding of endangered species, acquisition of habitat, research, education, and rehabilitation. A new raptor stamp and limited edition print is to be issued yearly, thus providing wildlife art collectors with additional materials to add to their collections.

DECOYS AND CARVINGS

Within recent years many birdwatchers also have discovered the enjoyment that can be derived from collecting bird decoys and carvings of one type or another. Indeed, collecting (perhaps even making) decoys and carvings now is an established part of American bird lore among both birdwatchers and sportsmen. In large measure, it was the latter who began serious decoy collecting, not too many years after market hunting of waterfowl and shorebirds was halted in 1918 in the United States by the enactment of the Migratory Bird Treaty.

What was collected after the end of market hunting was a treasure of unique Americana that finally is recognized for its artistic and financial value. Thus waterfowl, shorebird, and other decoys from the golden age of working decoy making now are almost priceless collector's items. They command many thousands of dollars at auctions, sales, exhibitions, and in antique shops.

Because of the rareness, physical size, and value of old working decoys, experienced collectors strongly recommend that new collectors follow a course of specialization when deciding what to collect. For example, one might buy only original New England (perhaps Cape Cod) or New Jersey shorebird decoys; or only mergansers; or only loons; or specific factory decoys. The list, of course, is long regarding which types of special decoys might be selected. Nevertheless, there are several advantages for entering into such specialization—the amount of space needed to store one's collection remains within reasonable requirements, funds can be used to purchase only the very finest and rarest decoys available, and one can become an authority on the area of specialization, thus greatly reducing the risk of buying a fake, restored, or inferior item because of ignorance.

This latter aspect of working decoy collecting is particularly important to novice collectors, although all collectors must remain alert to the possibility of fakes, alterations, or other inferior decoys being offered for sale by some persons. Therefore, among the features to look for when attempting to determine the authenticity of an old hunting decoy are specks of new glue where heads from one decoy were placed on bodies of another, new nail holes recently filled, or newly repainted decoys sometimes indi-

A variety of working decoys from the collection of the Shelburne Museum, Shelburne Vermont. Photo courtesy of the Shelburne Museum.

cated by the smell of fresh paint. Most importantly, never hesitate to lift a decoy and look at its underside to determine if original paint still remains (due to less wear) under the bill, head, and lead weight. More subjective, but vitally important is the need to study and learn to recognize the style used by the master carvers. This can be done in various museums containing authentic examples of decoys from the master carvers. Unfortunately there is no quick or easy way to develop this skill, so vital to successful working decoy collecting. Do not hesitate to seek experienced assistance, therefore, when buying expensive decoys if you have not yet mastered the basics needed to evaluate decoys correctly.

Because of the high cost of the finest and rarest examples of working decoys, and the difficulty of obtaining quality examples, many decoy collectors now focus their efforts upon collecting newly carved decorative decoys. Indeed, quality decorative decoys now are recognized as folk art forms in their own right—as the prices of the finest of these decoys and carvings demonstrate! However, it is quite possible to purchase many splendid examples of decorative decoys and carvings at relatively modest prices, often less than one hundred dollars, at all of the decoy and carving exhibitions held every year in various parts of the country. Waterfowl, shorebirds, and birds of prey are the most popular species fashioned with skill and care in wood, but sometimes other birds and animals are available too. Styles and quality of workmanship vary greatly, so one must select that which appeals best to himself or herself.

Hunting (Working) Decoys

As the name suggests, hunting or working decoys are hand-carved, wood models of waterfowl, shorebirds, and a variety of other species of birds made during the days of commercial or market hunting and used by market hunters to lure birds into shooting range. Some are more than one-hundred years old and many are at least seventy-five years old.

After one becomes interested in collecting hunting decoys, it becomes clear that the types of such decoys are representative of several major groups of birds. Moreover, there are numerous regional and individual craftsmen differences representative for many of these bird groups. In short, the hobby of collecting hunting decoys is complex, but fascinating, as is well described and illustrated in *American Bird Decoys* by William J. Mackey, Jr. It is worthwhile, therefore, to provide a short overview of each of the major bird groups for which hunting decoys have been identified, along with comments about the impact of the various regional aspects of these decoys.

Loon decoys that are old are extremely rare and valuable. Thus they are valued items in any hunting decoy collection. Generally such decoys were made in New England or the Canadian Maritime Provinces, more as a labor of love than as a needed hunting decoy. Because loon decoys were rarely made, each is a unique collector's item. Not infrequently they are heavy and crude, as well as being subject to rapid deterioration. A few are even made of loon skin, but most apparently were carved from wood.

During the days of uncontrolled hunting, late in the last century and early in this one, some hunters used decoys of various egrets and herons to lure birds into shooting range. The birds that were killed, including Great Blue Herons, Common Egrets, and Snowy Egrets were shot for food rather than for their feathers (plumage hunters shot the birds on their breeding rookeries, when the plumage was at its finest, without the use of decoys). In any event, Great Blue Heron hunting decoys were used both on the wetlands of Long Island and along coastal New Jersey. In a similar manner, hunting decoys of Common Egrets also were used along the coastlines of the Middle Atlantic states. However, these birds were then extremely rare, indeed nearly exterminated, thus decoys of Common Egrets were not used to any significant degree, which makes them very rare items. Nevertheless, some extremely attractive examples are known from the vicinity of Cape May, New Jersey. Even rarer, however, are Snowy Egret decoys which are known to have been made and used by hunters from Long Island southward to the Carolinas.

Waterfowl decoys, however, are the most common types of all hunting decoys and are the most widely and avidly collected among decoy enthusiasts. The variety of such decoys—in terms of species represented—is very substantial, even before one considers variations among the famous master carvers and regional differences in style. According to William J. Mackey, Jr., in his fine book *American Bird Decoys,* the following species are known to be represented as waterfowl hunting decoys.

Whistling Swan	Canvasback
Canada Goose	Greater Scaup
Brant	Lesser Scaup
Snow Goose (white phase)	Common Goldeneye
Snow Goose (blue phase)	Bufflehead
Mallard	Oldsquaw
American Black Duck	Common Eider
Gadwall	White-winged Scoter
Common Pintail	Surf Scoter
Green-winged Teal	Black Scoter
Blue-winged Teal	Ruddy Duck
American Wigeon	Labrador Duck
Northern Shoveler	Hooded Merganser
Wood Duck	Common Merganser

Redhead   Red-breasted Merganser
                        Ring-necked Duck

As one might expect, the master decoy makers generally carved decoys of those species of waterfowl that were most common in their particular geographic area. Thus Oldsquaw decoys, for example, were not uncommon along coastal New England but were rarely (if ever) made in some other areas. This geographic distribution of waterfowl, as reflected in which species were made as decoys, played an important role in the development of various "schools" of decoy making in different sections of the United States. Therefore, it is worthwhile to discuss some aspects of these regional decoy-making schools.

The hunting decoy makers of New England were well-known and respected craftsmen who produced many masterpieces over the years. On Monhegan Island, Maine, for example, some remarkable White-winged Scoter hunting decoys were produced and are now eagerly desired by avid collectors. Similarly, the superb decoys of Elmer Crowell of Cape Cod, Massachusetts, are among the most valuable and prized hunting decoys of any produced in the country. Those of Joseph Lincoln, and various other Massachusetts decoy makers, are also outstanding examples of the finest in the New England school of work. Farther south, in Connecticut, the work of Albert Laing of Stratford is recognized universally for its masterful quality. Laing was noted especially for his American Black Duck and Greater Scaup decoys, many of which are marked on the bottom with LAING burned into the wood. Other noted Stratford decoy makers include Benjamin Holmes and Charles E. Wheeler.

New York State, both coastal and inland, also produced a wide variety of hunting decoys of interest to collectors. On Long Island, for example, many fine waterfowl decoys were carved by such craftsmen as John Lee Baldwin, Thomas H. Gelston, George Pennell, Nelson Verity, and Charles Wheeler. Inland, in upstate New York, other decoy makers produced plenty of products, but generally of much lower quality than was made by the so-called "Long Island School" of carvers. Exceptions, however, are found in the work of such St. Lawrence River carvers as Samuel Denney, Frank Combs, and Chauncey Wheeler.

New Jersey also had its share of outstanding decoy makers whose work now is of great interest to collectors. In the Barnegat Bay area, for instance, the better-known carvers included Ben Hance—known especially for his Canvasback decoys—and Taylor Johnson. Ezra Hankins, however, made mostly American Black Duck, Redhead, and Greater Scaup decoys. Tom Gaskill, from Toms River, produced Redheads and a few other species. Other well-known decoy carvers include Lou Barkelow, Henry and Stanley Grant, and Alonzo and Sam Soper. Noted for splendid goose decoys was Jess Birdsall. Harry V. Shourdes, of Tuckerton, was equally masterful as a maker of Canada Geese, Brant, American Black Ducks, various diving ducks, and Red-breasted Mergansers. Another famous carver from Tuckerton was Samuel Smith. New Jersey also produced such well-known carvers as Lloyd Parker, Jed Sprague, Bradford Salmon, Roland Horner, and Joe King. Thus the decoy collector will find much fine material available from this important waterfowl state.

The lower Delaware River valley, from Trenton southward, also produced some fine decoy makers from both New Jersey and Pennsylvania. The duck decoys of this area are noted especially for their lifelike appearance and painting. Among the better of such decoys are those made by John Blair, Charles Black, John Dawson, and Ed and Jack Truland. Because these decoys were used in freshwater many still are preserved in much better condition than decoys used in brackish or saltwater.

Birdwatchers and decoy collectors alike also know well the importance of the lower Susquehanna River and Upper Chesapeake Bay areas as major waterfowl areas. Maryland, in particular, was well known as a major center for fine hunting-decoy making by such craftsmen as Howlett, Dye, Mitchell, McGaw, and Currier. The finest Chesapeake decoys, however, came from the shops of the famous carvers of Crisfield, of which Steve and Lemuel Ward stand above all the rest as the finest of decoy makers. All interested decoy collectors, therefore, will want to visit the fine Wildfowl Museum of the Ward Foundation at Salisbury State College, Maryland and enjoy the exhibits of many Ward brothers' decoys.

The eastern shore of Virginia is equally important to waterfowl and decoy makers and collectors (to say nothing of birdwatchers). The decoys made on Cobb Island, for example, are famous and desirable—especially those made by Nathan Cobb and marked with an initialed N on the decoy. Another Cobb Island carver of significance was John Hoff. In other sections of Virginia's eastern shore, decoy makers such as Walter Brady (noted for goose decoys), Ira Hudson of Chincoteague (who produced commercial decoys), Douglas Jester, David Watson, and Dan Whealton are important craftsmen.

The Back Bay section of Virginia, along with Carolina's Currituck Sound and the Outer Banks also produced outstanding hunting decoys now prized in any collection. Thus one finds rare, superb Whistling Swan decoys from John Williams of Cedar Island, Virginia, or the duck decoys of Lee and Lem Dudley with "L. D." burned into the bottoms of the decoys. Of course, there were other decoy makers of note as well in North Carolina and the area provides rich pickings for the serious collector.

Important as the Atlantic coastline is to decoy collectors, other great waterfowl areas of the United States—especially the famous Mississippi flyway—also produced fine decoy makers whose work is of great interest and value to collectors, although perhaps less so than the best of the famous Atlantic Coast decoys. Nevertheless, quality duck decoys from the mid-West do exist, but almost all were made after 1880 by such carvers as Robert A. Elliston, Kenneth Greenlee, Charles H. Perdew, Charles Walker, G. Bert Graves, and others. These are the men who produced the finest examples of the mid-Western decoys of Mallards, Common Pintails, Blue-winged Teal, Canvasbacks, Redheads, and a few other species—the decoys generally collected from that region by today's collectors.

During the days of market hunting, shorebirds were shot just as avidly and extensively as were ducks and other species of waterfowl. As a result, the market hunters made extensive use of shorebird decoys of about twenty different species, including the Eskimo Curlew which now is almost extinct. These old shorebird decoys, like their waterfowl counterparts, now are just as valuable and eagerly collected because of their splendid artistic quality and value. Superb, indeed, are the finest examples of the old decoys of godwits, curlews, yellowlegs, plovers, and other species from the various sections of our Atlantic coastline between New England and the Carolinas. And, as one might expect, many of the famous makers of waterfowl decoys are just as well known for their shorebird decoys. Thus the birdwatcher with a special interest in shorebirds might well consider collecting a few fine examples of old shorebird decoys simply for their artistic values. They are delightful items to have in one's home. *Shore Bird Decoys* by Henry A. Fleckenstein, Jr. is very helpful to shorebird decoy collectors.

In addition to the decoys already discussed, limited numbers of other decoys remaining from the days of market hunting also attract the attention of serious decoy collectors. Thus some remarkable decoys of terns, crows, owls, pigeons, flickers, and even blackbirds are known and highly valued among the unusual items one might strive to acquire. Common Tern decoys, for example, were made on Long Island's southern shore by at least one carver, but apparently at no other place. Although rare, Passenger Pigeon decoys also are known. Even rarer, but no less fascinating, are the few known Common (Yellow-shafted) Flicker decoys made only in Crisfield, Maryland. More common, however, are owl and crow decoys.

Factory Decoys

Long after the first hand carved decoys appeared in the United States, commercially produced decoys—the so-called factory decoys—appeared and were used by hunters. Many of these were made, at least in part, on a lathe although some also received final finishing by hand. Detroit, Michigan, became a center of manufacture of large numbers of factory decoys and a number of well-known companies now are recognized by decoy collectors. One such firm, for example, was the Dodge Decoy Factory owned by Jasper N. Dodge. The Dodge factory not only produced waterfowl decoys, but it also made various shorebirds and other made-to-order items.

The most important of the decoy factories, however, also of Detroit, was Mason's Decoy Factory which began production in 1899. Before long, Mason factory decoys were sold throughout

A preening yellow-legs carved by A. Elmer Crowell in the collection of the Shelburne Museum, Shelburne, Vermont. Photo courtesy of the Shelburne Museum.

America, and the Mason product became the most celebrated factory decoy in America. Like the Dodge Decoy Factory, the Mason firm produced waterfowl, shorebird, and other decoys, as well as occasional special order items. To the modern decoy collector, ownership of a top-of-the-brand Mason factory decoy in good condition—such as one of their splendid Wood Ducks—is not only a valuable item but also a fine example of workmanship.

Other companies also made decoys of various types that decoy collectors now find of interest and worthy of collecting. For example, the William E. Pratt Manufacturing Company produced duck and crow decoys, the Evans Decoy Factory produced Mallard decoys and a few other species, and the brothers Harvey and George Stevens of Weedsport, New York, also produced commercial decoys of high quality. In addition, many other smaller companies also manufactured factory decoys. *American Factory Decoys* by Henry A. Fleckenstein, Jr. is a helpful reference.

Decorative Decoys and Carvings

If birdwatchers think the art of making decoys vanished with the market hunters, a visit to any decoy show will destroy that idea immediately. Decoy making is as popular as ever, but decoys produced today are so-called decorative decoys. The very best are full-size, lifelike models of the subject valued as much as $10,000 each! Collecting decorative decoys now is in vogue and continues to become increasingly popular.

While various species of waterfowl form a major subject area for decorative decoy makers and collectors, shorebirds and other species of North American birds—and even mammals such as whales—also are made as decorative decoys. At one show on the eastern shore of Maryland, for example, I saw a spectacular life-size carved Osprey in flight, along with many perched birds of prey. A variety of such examples are exhibited at the Wildfowl Museum in Maryland, and others also are on exhibit at the National Carvers Museum in Colorado.

Some of the work produced by decorative decoy makers and carvers is spectacular. Rare is the birdwatcher visiting a show such as the Academy of Natural Sciences of Philadelphia's annual Wildfowl Art Expo who does not purchase at least one decoy for use at home! While the best of the decoys produced by our leading carvers are very expensive, there are other fine decoys also available from lesser-known carvers at more modest prices.

In addition to decorative decoys of game birds, there are many excellent bird carvers in the United States and Canada who make superb lifelike carvings of a wide variety of songbirds, birds of prey, shorebirds and other waterbirds, and mammals. Among the better-known decorative decoy carvers are Tom Ahern, Clarence Carlyle Ailes, Tad Beach, Charles R. Berry, Anneli Bonn and family, Donald Briddell, Robert Brophy, Dan Brown, Ed and Esther Burns, Bobby Castlebury, Bob Elliott, John Franco, J. B. Garton, Al Glassford, Jack and Betty Holt, Jim Hutcheson, Louis L. Kean, Jr., William J. Koelpin, Oliver J. Lawson, Richard LeMaster, Ernest Muehlmatt, John Mullican, David S. Murray, Robert Ptasknik, A. J. Rudisill, William L. Schultz, Bennett Scott, John T. Sharp, Gus Sjoholm, James Sprankle, Harold Vandyke, Donald Vassallo, William Veasey, Robert and Virginia Warfield, Herschel E. Westbrook, Dan Williams, and Phillip E. Zeller.

The team of Robert and Virginia Warfield of Jaffrey, New Hampshire, for example, is well known for the superb bird carvings which reflect natural history accuracy in all details. As a result of the quality of their craftsmanship, Warfield birds are collected widely and are appreciated for what they are—works of art reflecting the beauty of nature.

Much the same can be said of the splendid carvings of birds by Phillip E. Zeller of East Arlington, Vermont. They, too, are works of a master and widely collected and represented in various private and museum collections. The carvings of many of the other carvers just mentioned also are very fine and appreciated by all who see them.

DECOY AND CARVING MUSEUMS

Several museums in the United States own and exhibit large collections of hunting and/or decorative decoys and other bird carvings. Birdwatchers interested in this subject will find it worthwhile to visit these institutions to study and enjoy their decoy and carving exhibits. The museums listed here are especially recommended.

Many decorative bird decoys are spectacular. These Pileated Woodpeckers were carved by Robert and Virginia Warfield of Jaffrey, New Hampshire. Photo courtesy of Robert Warfield.

A Belted Kingfisher carved by Philip Zeller of East Arlington, Vermont. Photo courtesy of Phillip Zeller.

1,000 Islands Museum
401 Riverside Drive
Old Town Hall
Clayton, New York 13624

National Carvers Museum
Woodcarver Road
Monument, Colorado 80132

The Shelburne Museum, Inc.
U. S. Route 7
Shelburne, Vermont 05482

Wildfowl Museum of the Ward Foundation
c/o Salisbury State College
Salisbury, Maryland 21801

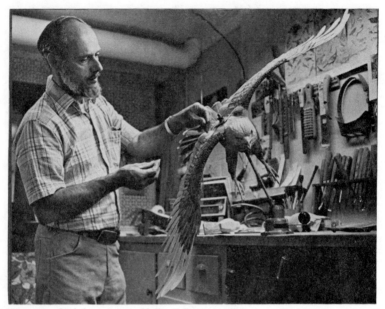

Decorative bird decoy carver Phillip Zeller at work on a carving. Photo courtesy of Phillip Zeller.

Of these institutions, the Shelburne Museum in Vermont is of great interest and importance because it houses one of the largest and most comprehensive collections of American decoys exhibited anywhere. Approximately 2,000 birds from crude stickups to reed decoys to splendid carvings by masters such as A. Elmer Crowell, Joseph Lincoln, Harry B. Shourdes, and "Shang" Wheeler are included. Most of the decoys date from the period 1850–1918, and many are from the famed collections of Joel Barber, Richard H. Moeller, Edward H. Mulliken, and William Mackey.

The Wildfowl Museum in Maryland also is of great interest and importance. It is devoted exclusively to exhibiting and collecting hunting and decorative decoys and other bird carvings. Particular emphasis is placed on the work of the famed Ward brothers (for whom the Ward Foundation is named) and their superb decoys, but the works of numerous other craftsmen are represented, including exhibits illustrating the history of decoy making and use. Thus a visit to the Wildfowl Museum is most worthwhile.

ART AND LIMITED EDITION PRINTS

Just as the number of people swelling the ranks of birdwatchers has increased enormously in this Age of Bird Watching, so too has the number of outstanding bird and wildlife artists increased considerably in recent years. As a result, a considerable quantity of original bird art—sketches, drawings, oil paintings, and watercolor paintings—now are available for birdwatchers and wildlife art collectors who wish to invest money in these beautiful art productions. How much money one invests varies greatly depending upon many factors not the least important of which is the reputation of the artist. An original bird painting by Roger Tory Peterson would sell for many thousands of dollars, but lesser-known artists—sometimes young painters with developing skills and more limited reputations—sell their work for much less money. Thus any birdwatcher wishing to own an original painting of birds can do so, often for a few hundred dollars, if they select the work of lesser-known (but nevertheless talented) artists. In my own collection, for example, I have various paintings from the brush of Rod Arbogast—a young Pennsylvania wildlife artist who prepared some of the illustrations published in several of my books—as well as work by several nationally known artists.

Although any original artwork from the brush of a talented artist is valuable, original paintings that are reproduced in books or used for the preparation of limited edition prints take on added value and are even more desirable to collectors. On the other hand, birdwatchers wishing to own fine limited edition prints from even the most famous bird and wildlife artists can do so readily and for much less money than one must spend to purchase original paintings. Signed and numbered limited edition prints now are readily available, often for less than one hundred dollars, from numerous galleries and print dealers across America. They are not only extremely attractive for use in home or office, but frequently represent good financial investments since most prints rapidly increase in value after the edition is sold out. Of particular

Roger Tory Peterson is America's best known bird artist. His original paintings, and limited edition prints, are valuable collector's items. Photo courtesy of Roger Tory Peterson.

Wildlife artist Ned Smith in his studio. His paintings and limited edition prints are major collector's items to wildlife art enthusiasts. Photo courtesy of Ned Smith.

importance to many collectors are prints made from the paintings used on the federal duck stamps and the Wild Turkey stamps issued by the National Wild Turkey Federation. There is a keen market for such offerings.

In addition to regular limited edition signed and numbered prints, there are at least two special features found on some such prints that add to their value. One feature is known as a remarque—a small, original sketch or painting done by the artist on the border of the print. One thus has a fine print coupled with a miniature *original* work done by the artist. As one might expect, prints that are remarqued are much more valuable than those lacking it. They also are much rarer than regular limited edition signed and numbered prints.

The second special category for wildlife print collectors is the so-called artist's proof. It is one of a few limited edition prints, perhaps twenty or less, that the artist inspected during the early printing of a signed and numbered edition and is marked by the artist as an artist's proof. It also is signed by the artist. It may, or may not, be numbered but it is valued more than the regular signed and numbered prints in the issue and thus is something collectors seek to acquire if possible.

Still another type of bird or wildlife print—the so-called open edition print—is not numbered or limited in the number of copies printed. Generally these prints are not signed by the artist, but occasionally they are and may even be dated. Open edition prints are the least valuable, in most instances, but also sell for the least amount of money, thus making them available to a very wide audience.

Persons seriously interested in bird and wildlife art will find several excellent articles on various aspects of the subject included in several issues of *The Living Bird* published by the Cornell University Laboratory of Ornithology. These articles are included in the Additional Reading section at the end of this chapter.

AUTOGRAPHS

One of the more historical facets of collecting bird-related items is that of collecting autographs of famous birdwatchers and ornithologists. The easiest and least expensive time to develop such collections is while the people are still alive. Then it is frequently possible to obtain autographs for the price of a postage stamp and request. Generally, however, such autographs are less valuable than those from persons no longer living.

The number of persons whose autographs are collectible material is large and growing yearly. Most valuable are autographs of the very famous naturalists such as John James Audubon and Alexander Wilson, but autographs of lesser-known birdwatchers and ornithologists can be purchased in many instances from recognized autograph dealers. Thus it is possible still to obtain material from such persons as Louis Agassiz Fuertes, Arthur Cleveland Bent, Robert Cushman Murphy, and Frank M. Chapman.

Several books including Ernest A. Choate's *The Dictionary of American Bird Names,* Edward S. Gruson's *Words for Birds,* John K. Terres' *The Audubon Society Encyclopedia of North American Birds,* and my own *The Illustrated Bird Watcher's Dic-*

tionary provide collectors with basic lists of past important ornithologists and some birdwatchers whose autographs might be desirable in one's collection. The following list contains the names of the most important of such persons, along with the years during which they lived.

Abert, James William (1820–1897)
Allen, Arthur Augustus (1885–1964)
Allen, Charles Andrew (1841–1930)
Allen, Joel Asaph (1838–1921)
Allen, Robert Porter (1905–1963)
Audubon, John James (1785–1851)
Bachman, John (1790–1874)
Bailey, Florence Merriam (1863–1928)
Bailey, Harry Balch (1853–1928)
Baird, Spencer Fullerton (1823–1887)
Baldwin, Samuel Prentiss (1868–1938)
Barbour, Thomas (1884–1946)
Bartram, William (1739–1823)
Beck, Herbert Huebener (1875–1960)
Beebe, Charles William (1877–1962)
Bendire, Charles Emil (1836–1897)
Bent, Arthur Cleveland (1866–1954)
Brewer, Thomas Mayo (1814–1880)
Brewster, William (1851–1919)
Broley, Charles L. (?–1959)
Broun, Maurice (1906–1979)
Burleigh, Thomas Dearborn (1895–1973)
Burroughs, John (1837–1921)
Cabot, Samuel (1815–1885)
Carson, Rachel (1907–1964)
Cassin, John (1813–1869)
Chapin, James Paul (1889–1964)
Chapman, Frank Michler (1864–1945)
Clark, William (1770–1838)
Cooper, William C. (1798–1864)
Cory, Charles Barney (1857–1921)
Coues, Elliott (1842–1899)
Cruickshank, Allan D. (1907–1974)

Deignan, Herbert Girton (1906–1968)
Dwight, Jonathan (1858–1929)
Errington, Paul Lester (1902–1962)
Fisher, Albert Kenrick (1856–1948)
Forbush, Edward Howe (1858–1929)
Fuertes, Louis Agassiz (1874–1927)
Gambel, William (1819–1849)
Gillespie, John A. (1893–1956)
Gilliard, E. Thomas (1912–1965)
Grinnell, George Bird (1849–1938)
Grinnell, Joseph (1877–1939)
Griscom, Ludlow (1890–1959)
Gross, Alfred Otto (1883–1970)
Harlan, Richard (1796–1843)
Harlow, Richard C. (1889–1962)
Harper, Francis (1886–1972)
Heermann, Adolphus L. (1818–1865)
Henshaw, Henry Wetherbee (1850–1930)
Herrick, Francis Hobart (1858–1940)
Howell, Arthur H. (1872–1940)
Jacobs, Joseph A. (1917–1977)
Jaques, Francis Lee (1887–1969)
Jewett, Stanley Gordon (1885–1955)
Jones, Lynds (1865–1951)
Kalmbach, Edwin Richard (1884–1972)
Kirtland, Jared Potter (1793–1877)
Land, Hugh Colman (1929–1968)
Lawrence, George Newbold (1806–1895)
Lewis, Meriwether (1774–1809)
Lincoln, Frederick (1892–1960)
Linsdale, Jean Myron (1902–1969)
Loomis, Leverett Mills (1857–1928)
Low, Seth Haskell (1911–1962)
Lucas, Frederick Augustus (1852–1929)
McAtee, W. L. (1883–1962)
Merriam, Clinton Hart (1855–1942)
Miller, Alden Holmes (1906–1965)
Miller, Loye Holmes (1874–1970)
Miller, Waldron De Witt (1879–1929)

Moore, Robert Thomas (1882–1958)
Murphy, Robert Cushman (1887–1973)
Nice, Margaret Morse (1883–1974)
Nuttall, Thomas (1786–1859)
Oberholser, Harry Church (1870–1963)
Osgood, Wilfred Hudson (1875–1947)
Palmer, Theodore Sherman (1868–1955)
Peters, James Lee (1889–1952)
Phelps, William Henry (1875–1965)
Phillips, John Charles (1876–1938)
Poole, Earl Lincoln (1891–1972)
Rhoads, Samuel Nicholson (1863–1952)
Ridgway, Robert (1850–1929)
Roberts, Thomas Sadler (1858–1946)
Rogers, Charles Henry (1888–1977)
Rowan, William (1891–1957)
Saunders, Aretas Andrews (1884–1970)
Schorger, Arlie William (1884–1972)
Shufeldt, Robert Wilson (1850–1934)
Sprunt, Alexander, Jr. (1898–1973)
Stoddard, Herbert Lee (1889–1968)
Stone, Witmer (1866–1939)
Strong, Reuben Myron (1872–1964)
Tarber, Wendell (1897–1960)
Taverner, Percy Algernon (1875–1947)
Thayer, John Eliot (1862–1933)
Todd, Walter Edmund Clyde (1874–1969)
Townsend, Charles Haskins (1859–1944)
Townsend, John Kirk (1809–1851)
Turnbull, William P. (1830–1871)
Van Tyne, Josselyn (1902–1956)
Vaurie, Charles (1906–1975)
Wayne, Arthur Trezevant (1863–1930)
Wetmore, Alexander (1886–1978)
Wilson, Alexander (1766–1813)

For an up-to-date list of contemporary ornithologists one can do no better than consult the membership list of the Ornithological Societies of North America, available from the American Ornithologists' Union. It contains thousands of names and addresses of ornithologists living in the Americas.

Limited numbers of names and addresses of persons in various foreign countries also are included. Thus, among living ornithologists and birdwatchers, one would want to consider collecting autographs from such persons as Roger Tory Peterson and Olin Sewall Pettingill, Jr. who have become well-known public figures through the publication of their various books, lectures, and other activities involved with birds and wildlife.

In addition to knowing which ornithologists and birdwatchers are possible figures whose autographs one might wish to collect, it also is important to know some of the basics of autograph collecting. An excellent book to begin with is Charles Hamilton's *The Book of Autographs* because it provides expert recommendations to beginners.

Among the basics one should master is an understanding of the standard abbreviations and meanings of the terms used by philographers (autograph collectors). Thus an autograph, for example, refers to anything that is written by hand and not simply a person's signature. Letters, manuscripts, diaries, and other handwritten documents all are considered autographs. The following abbreviations also are important.

Sig. Refers to a person's signature.

DS. Refers to a document signed by the writer but perhaps typed or handwritten by another person.

LS. Refers to a letter that is signed by the writer but perhaps typed or handwritten by another person for the person signing the letter.

ALS. Refers to a letter written and signed by the writer. The term means autograph letter signed.

AQS. Means autograph quotation signed. Generally it is a statement or verse written and signed by the author.

SP. Refers to a signed photograph.

The financial value of an autograph also is of more than minor interest to most collectors. Thus it is important to understand what makes an autograph valuable. To begin, age in itself does not necessarily bring value to an autograph. Rareness, demand, and content influence value greatly. Thus important and interesting letters usually increase an autograph's value. Handwritten rather than typed letters tend to bring increased value to an autograph, especially when most letters from a particular person are usually typed. For the most part, however, most autographs from ornithologists and birdwatchers have limited financial value and should be collected for pleasure and enjoyment. Exceptions, of course, are autographs from people like John James Audubon and a few other noted persons of historic importance. In a similar manner, autographs from authors of books about birds would generally be slightly more valuable than from persons who have not written books.

POSTCARDS

Collecting postcards featuring paintings or photographs of birds is another facet of collecting bird-related items in which birdwatchers sometimes participate. It is, generally, a very inexpensive hobby to be enjoyed at leisure whenever a new postcard is offered for sale at nature centers or other places where birds and other wildlife are featured.

Bird postcards are separated into two types—commercially printed issues and homemade photographic cards. Commercial cards are available in almost endless variety. In my own collection, for example, numerous families of birds are represented with such varied species shown as Northern Gannets at Bonaventure Island, Quebec, Golden Eagles aloft over Hawk Mountain, Pennsylvania, and Waved Albratrosses on Hood Island, Galapagos. Privately made bird postcards are much rarer and usually are unique. They commonly feature some exceptionally attractive black and white bird photograph taken by the person making the card.

I know of no formal catalog of bird postcards such as one can refer to for postage or federal duck stamps. Nevertheless, one simply should try to acquire as many different cards as possible, of any many different species as possible, using any of the checklists of the world's birds as a guide to which species might be represented on cards. I simply buy cards when I see them and recognize them as not being represented in my collection. Sometimes friends also send me cards when they see them and think I may not have such issues already.

A variety of postcards of pictures of birds from the author's collection.

EMBROIDERED SHOULDER PATCHES

Most bird clubs and Audubon societies in the United States and Canada sell embroidered cloth patches featuring the name of their organization and its symbol. Such shoulder patches are extremely popular items and many birdwatchers sew them onto jackets, field packs, or other outdoor packs. Until now, however, few (if any) birdwatchers have begun collections of such patches, although some are extremely colorful and attractive. Therefore why not collect such patches from as many organizations as possible? With more than 1,000 bird clubs in the United States and Canada, one can obtain a large collection of shoulder patches easily. Older, now obsolete patches, formerly used by organizations but replaced with new ones with different designs, expand still further the scope and possibility of such materials.

As an adjunct to a collection of bird club patches, it would be worthwhile to try to obtain some brief history of the club and its patch including the name of the person who designed it, the first year the patch became available to the public, and the length of time it remained available. Such background information would be invaluable in the future to anybody interested in writing an article or book about bird club patch collecting or preparing an illustrated catalog of such patches, such as has been done for American military insignia and related items.

ADDITIONAL READING

Academy of Natural Sciences
   1981   *Wildfowl Art Expo*. Academy of Natural Sciences of Philadelphia, Philadelphia, Pa.
Anonymous
   1972   National Wildlife Federation: The Dream that Stamps Built. *National Wildlife*, 10 (6): 26–27, 30, 32. October–November issue.
   1978   *Duck Stamp Data*. Circular 111. U. S. Fish and Wildlife Service, Washington, D. C.
   1979a Federal Duck Stamp Collecting Grows Steadily, *Prints*, 1 1(2): 58–60.
   1979b The Artist—Albert Earl Gilbert. *Prints*, 1 (2): 14, 16–19, 48.
Barber, J.
   1954   *Wild Fowl Decoys*. Dover Publications, Inc., New York, N. Y.
Boynton, M. F.
   1956   *Louis Agassiz Fuertes: His Life Briefly Told and His Correspondence*. Oxford University Press, New York, N. Y.
Cheever, B.
   1971   *Ward Brothers*. North American Decoys, Heber City, Utah.
Devlin, J. C. and G. Naismith
   1977   *The World of Roger Tory Peterson*. Time Books, New York, N. Y.
Earnest, A.
   1965   *The Art of the Decoys*. Bramhall House, New York, N. Y.
Eckelberry, D. R.
   1963   Birds in Art and Illustration. *Living Bird*, 2: 69–82.
   1965   Techniques in Bird Illustration. *Living Bird*, 4: 131–160.
Fink, R. A.
   1977   *A Catalog of the Wild Turkey Stamp Prints with Biographies of the Artists*. Privately published, Lorton, Va.
Fleckenstein, H. A., Jr.
   1979   *Decoys of the Mid-Atlantic Region*. Schiffer Publishing Ltd., Exton, Pa.
   1980   *Shore Bird Decoys*. Schiffer Publishing Ltd., Exton, Pa.
   1981   *American Factory Decoys*. Schiffer Publishing Ltd., Exton, Pa.

Hamilton, C.
    1978   *The Book of Autographs.* Simon and Schuster, New York,
            N. Y.
Hatcher, J. B. (Ed.)
    1979   *Scott Specialized Catalogue of United States Stamps 1980.*
            Fifty-eighth Edition. Scott Publishing Co., New York, N. Y.
Mackey, W. J., Jr.
    1965   *American Bird Decoys.* E. P. Dutton & Co., Inc., New York,
            N. Y.
McCormick, L.
    1980   Man-Made Birds. *Bird Watcher's Digest,* 2 (5): 40–44.
Mengel, R. M.
    1980   Beauty and the Beast: Natural History and Art. *Living Bird,*
            18: 27–70.
Reiger, G.
    1977   The Treasure of Wildlife Stamps. *Field & Stream,* LXXXII
            (2): 114–116, 118–120, 126–127. June issue.
Small, A.
    1981   *Masters of Decorative Bird Carving.* Winchester Press, Tulsa,
            Oklahoma.
Stanley, W. F. *et al*
    1974   *Birds of the World on Stamps.* Handbook No. 82. American
            Topical Association, Milwaukee, Wisc.
Starr, G. R., Jr.
    1974   *Decoys of the Atlantic Flyway.* Winchester Press, Inc., Tulsa,
            Oklahoma.
Sutton, G. M.
    1962   Is Bird-Art Art? *Living Bird,* 1: 73–78.
    1979   *To a Young Bird Artist/Letters from Louis Agassiz Fuertes
            to George Miksch Sutton.* University of Oklahoma Press,
            Norman, Oklahoma.

Chapter 10

Locally Endangered Species Projects

During recent years a great deal of governmental and private interest in endangered species of birds and other wildlife and plantlife has developed in the United States and elsewhere. Millions of dollars now are spent on projects designed to prevent endangered species from falling into the pit of extinction. Almost all of these efforts deal with those species that are considered endangered on an international, national, or state level. Usually neglected are species that are only locally endangered.

These are species whose survival as a resident or breeding species in a county is in jeopardy. Their unfortunate status may result from change in habitat, loss of habitat, over-exploitation by man, use of pesticides, predation, disease, undesirable interspecific competition, because the county is an isolated outpost for the species, because the species live in the county at the extreme edge of their range, or other factors. Usually a locally endangered species is *not* endangered throughout the broad extent of its geographic range. Nevertheless, locally endangered species are so reduced in numbers *in a county* that they could become exterminated there. Thus part of an area's local wildlife heritage would be lost. In some instances preservation and protection of habitat can prevent this from happening.

Because locally endangered species are mostly of local concern they can provide the basis for various special restoration projects for bird clubs and other interested birdwatchers with limited resources available to them. In short, why not organize local talents and efforts and establish local endangered species projects? Such projects can provide extremely worthwhile wildlife conservation experiences, stimulate local interest and pride in an area's birdlife and other wildlife, and provide interested participants with experience and skills useful also for application to state and national conservation efforts. In addition, concern about locally endangered species may stimulate local governmental officials to include serious consideration of the rights of wildlife and plantlife in their various activities and actions.

LOCAL ENDANGERED SPECIES LISTS

The first step in developing a local endangered species project is the preparation of a list of species that are locally endangered. A county is an appropriate geographic area to cover. To prepare such a list the federal list of endangered species should be consulted first. It appears in numerous parts in the *Federal Register*, with additional details published in the *Endangered Species Technical Bulletin* issued monthly by the United States Fish and Wildlife Service. Those federally endangered species that occur in your county are the first to be placed on your local endangered species list.

Next consult your state list of endangered species if one is available from your state's wildlife agency. Add any species included on that list to your local list if they occur in your county.

Finally conduct a complete review of local data to evaluate the current resident or breeding status of birds in your county. Particularly important sources of information include publications on the county's birdlife, data on sets of bird eggs collected in the past in the county and preserved in local or state museums, unpublished field notes of competent local birdwatchers, and critical

Black-crowned Night Herons are among the species that suffer habitat loss due to wetland destruction. Thus they may become locally endangered.

general evaluations of the local species in the county by persons with at least ten years of active local birding experience. Based upon all of these sources, it is possible to prepare a list of species whose local breeding populations clearly are drastically reduced or nearly eliminated in numbers. They are the species to be included on the locally endangered species list. Here are several examples of the species write-ups for locally endangered birds in Lehigh County, Pennsylvania.

"RED-HEADED WOODPECKER (*Melanerpes erythrocephalus*)
Status: ENDANGERED

Formerly nested near the Fish Hatchery and in northwestern Allentown in the early 1930's and 1940's. No recent nests are known. Habitat destruction and competition with Starlings seem to be partly responsible for the decline of this species."

"WHITE-EYED VIREO (*Vireo griseus*)

Status: ENDANGERED

Nested near Sigmund, Upper Milford Township, in 1954. Habitat destruction of that site may have eliminated the species as a breeding bird in the county."

PERMITS

Before starting work on a locally endangered species project, especially if the effort involves handling or marking birds, contact your state wildlife agency to determine if state permits are required to engage in the project being considered. Each state has different laws concerning wildlife, so it is not possible here to outline any particular restrictions or regulations. However, full details can be obtained from the various wildlife agencies whose addresses are listed in the appendix.

In addition to necessary state permits, some projects also require federal permits issued by the United States Fish and Wildlife Service. Further information can be obtained by contacting one of the regional offices of this agency whose addresses are listed here.

Regional Director U. S. Fish and Wildlife Service 1011 E. Tudor Road Anchorage, Alaska 99503

Regional Director U. S. Fish and Wildlife Service 500 N. E. Multnomah St. Portland, Oregon 97232

Regional Director U. S. Fish and Wildlife Service 500 Gold Avenue, SW Albuquerque, New Mexico 87103

Regional Director U. S. Fish and Wildlife Service Federal Building Fort Snelling Twin Cities, Minnesota 55111

Regional Director U. S. Fish and Wildlife Service 75 Spring St., SW Atlanta, Georgia 30303

Regional Director U. S. Fish and Wildlife Service One Gateway Center, Suite 700 Newton Corner, Massachusetts 02158

Regional Director U. S. Fish and Wildlife Service 134 Union Blvd. Denver, Colorado 80225

Regardless of the types of permits that may be needed to conduct certain bird studies, it is vital that birdwatchers engaged in such projects obtain all necessary permits and permissions *before* work begins. It also is vital that required annual reports, or other documents required by governmental agencies, be completed properly and filed with the necessary agencies *when they are due*. Failure to do so can put worthwhile conservation programs in jeopardy.

TYPES OF PROJECTS

As soon as a list of locally endangered species is prepared, it is possible to consider restoration projects that can be developed to aid some of the species on the list. Keep in mind, however, that it may not be possible to aid every species on the list. For some, perhaps no obvious cause for the local decline in numbers can be determined. For others, perhaps very complex causes are responsible for the species becoming locally endangered and the remedial action needed to offset those causes exceptionally complex, technically difficult, or very costly. But for some, relatively simple or inexpensive actions might restore local populations of these birds to former numbers.

Here are some more specific types of actions suitable for bird clubs or interested persons to undertake if they want to provide assistance to locally endangered birds.

NEST BOXES

Construction and placement of nest boxes for selected species that accept boxes as nest sites when natural nest sites are lacking is one effective way in which birdwatchers can make a dramatic impact upon the breeding populations of some birds. It is not possible here to discuss all species of birds that use nest boxes, nor is there any point in doing so, since box or cavity nesting birds that are locally endangered will vary widely in various parts of the United States and Canada. Nevertheless, additional com-

Nest Box Dimensions

Species	Floor of Cavity	Depth of Cavity	Entrance above Floor	Diameter of Entrance	Height above Ground
	Inches	Inches	Inches	Inches	Feet
Eastern Bluebird	5×5	8	6	1½	5–10
American Robin	6×8	8	*	*	6–15
Black-capped Chickadee	4×4	8–10	6–8	1⅛	6–15
Tufted Titmouse	4×4	8–10	6–8	1¼	6–15
White-breasted Nuthatch	4×4	8–10	6–8	1¼	12–20
House Wren	4×4	6–8	1–6	1–1¼	6–10
Bewick's Wren	4×4	6–8	1–6	1–1¼	6–10
Carolina Wren	4×4	6–8	1–6	1½	6–10
Violet-green Swallow	5×5	6	1–5	1½	10–15
Tree Swallow	5×5	6–8	5–6	1½	6–16
Barn Swallow	6×6	6	*	*	8–12
Purple Martin	6×6	6	1	2½	15–20
Prothonotary Warbler	6×6	6	4	1½	2–4
European Starling	6×6	16–18	14–16	2	10–25
Eastern Phoebe	6×6	6	*	*	9–12
Great Crested Flycatcher	6×6	8–10	6–8	2	8–20
Common Flicker	7×7	16–18	14–16	2½	6–20
Golden-fronted Woodpecker	6×6	12–15	9–12	2	12–20
Red-headed Woodpecker	6×6	12–15	9–12	2	12–20
Downy Woodpecker	4×4	9–12	6–8	1¼	6–20
Hairy Woodpecker	6×6	12–15	9–12	1½	12–20
Screech Owl	8×8	12–15	9–12	3	10–30
Saw-whet Owl	6×6	10–12	8–10	2½	12–20
Barn Owl	10×18	15–18	4	6	12–18
American Kestrel	11×11	12	9–12	3×4	20–30
Wood Duck	10×18	10–24	12–16	4	10–20

Source: Homes for Birds, Conservation Bulletin 14, U. S. Fish and Wildlife Service, Washington, D. C.

*One or more sides are kept open.

ments on a few selected species that are widely reduced in numbers in much of the United States and Canada can be helpful. Certainly the various species of bluebirds of North America all can benefit greatly from the erection of bluebird nest box trails, and in those areas where such trails are established, there have generally been dramatic increases in local bluebird populations.

For persons seriously interested in helping bluebirds recover some of their former numbers by use of nest boxes, the essential reference for such work is Lawrence Zeleny's *The Bluebird*. It contains basic details for construction of boxes for all three species—Eastern Bluebird, Western Bluebird, and Mountain Bluebird—including tips on how to deal with other birds that also use bluebird boxes as uninvited guests. In addition, there are plans for the construction of bluebird winter roosting boxes which are very useful in providing these beautiful birds with protection and shelter from winter's cold weather. The very latest information on bluebirds and their conservation is available from the North American Bluebird Society, Box 6295, Silver Spring, Maryland 20906, which actively promotes bluebird conservation in North America.

One of the pleasant side benefits that result from the establishment of bluebird nest box trails is the use of many of these boxes by Tree Swallows, which are much more common birds than any of the bluebird species, but, nevertheless, very delightful creatures to have in an area. Tree Swallows use the boxes readily which, in some cases, may mean that some extra boxes must be used to provide the bluebirds with the maximum opportunity for occupation of nest sites. Most birdwatchers involved in bluebird conservation efforts do not object to the use of some boxes by swallows and various other species.

HABITAT PROTECTION

In many cases, loss of habitat is the primary reason why various species of birds and other wildlife are either locally endangered or endangered on a wider geographic area. Man and his endless activities have inflicted disastrous impacts upon many species, and it is now widely recognized by wildlife conservationists that

An Eastern Bluebird nesting in a cavity in a post. Loss of such sites can result in bluebirds becoming locally endangered. Use of bluebird boxes can help to provide needed homes for these birds.

Wildlife conservationist Barry Reed erecting a bluebird box at his home. Trails of such boxes in an area can be a major bluebird conservation project and prevent the birds from becoming locally endangered.

habitat protection and preservation is the first priority when trying to save a species. In the case of locally endangered species, habitat protection is no less an important factor. Thus every effort should be made to identify species that are locally endangered because of loss of habitat.

After identification of such birds, vigorous efforts can be undertaken to try to save essential or locally critical habitat so that the remaining representatives of the species can survive. In some instances, development of land may prevent saving necessary habitat. But in other instances detailed discussions of the needs of affected species with persons—governmental, industrial, commercial, or others—might lead to ways in which projects can be altered to accommodate the needs of locally endangered birds. Not infrequently persons involved with development projects are unfamiliar with the existence and requirements of locally endan-

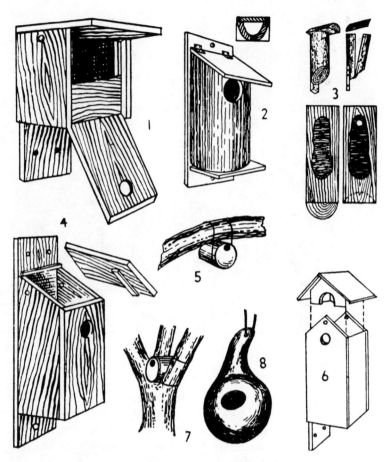

Variations on designs for bird houses. Reprinted from **Homes for Birds,** *Conservation Bulletin 14, U. S. Fish and Wildlife Service, Washington, D. C.*

gered species and do not realize the impact of their activities upon wildlife. Certainly discussions with project owners or managers can do no harm and might result in the protection and preservation of vital habitat.

When such discussions are held, it is important to present more than opinions. Well-documented conclusions based upon accurate

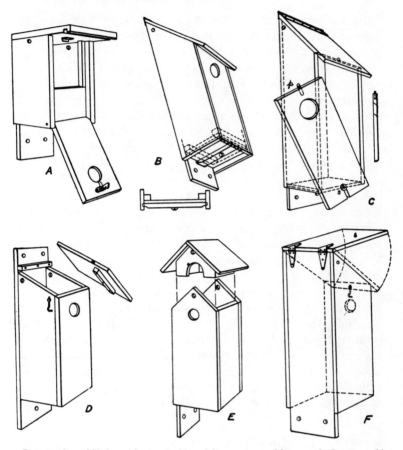

Construction of bird next boxes. A, hinged front supported by a catch; B, removable bottom, released via turn of a cleat; C, swinging front, held in place by a pin p and by tightening screw s; D and E, removable tops; F, hinged top. Reprinted from Homes for Birds, Conservation Bulletin 14, U. S. Fish and Wildlife Service, Washington, D. C.

field studies and citations of the published work of other ornithologists present a much more effective approach to meetings with developers who generally are economically oriented and have little appreciation for wildlife and its survival needs. But when faced with solid scientific data to support one's discussion, developers find it more difficult to dismiss objections to projects. It is then that some provisions might be made to save wildlife habitat.

It also is helpful if professional ornithologists or wildlife biologists can assist in the presentation of requests for the protection and preservation of locally critical wildlife habitat. Generally such persons have considerably more experience dealing with public hearings, formal discussions, and generally defending the needs of birds and wildlife. Thus efforts should be made to enlist the aid of such professionals if they are available locally.

Among the habitat types that are especially vulnerable to reckless destruction are wetlands used by waterbirds and waterfowl. When sites involving these birds are threatened, especially if large numbers of nesting birds are involved, special efforts should be made to save them. In many sections of the United States, coastline atlases of all known nesting colonies are already available from the United States Fish and Wildlife Service (see Chapter 4). Such information should be used at once if colonial nesting waterbird colonies are involved in habitat alteration plans in a county. Certainly when the breeding sites of such birds are threatened, state or National Audubon Society representatives, as well as state and federal wildlife officials, should be made aware of the situations without delay. In addition, local or regional conservationists should be notified in the event they can obtain control of such lands and establish wildlife refuges.

HABITAT RESTORATION

In some instances, habitat is severely damaged or destroyed completely and thus is responsible for the locally endangered status of some species of birds. Nevertheless, it may be possible to restore damaged habitat, or even recreate habitat that is already gone.

Wetlands, for example, frequently are used as dumping sites for garbage and other trash. In some cases, however, it is possible to mount cleanup projects using concerned local citizens—it matters not if they are dedicated birdwatchers—and remove the rubbish, trash, and garbage from marshes or other types of wetlands. Provided that no serious chemical pollution is present, it might

Wetlands are especially vulnerable to destruction. Their loss can result in many waterbirds becoming locally endangered.

be possible to establish protection for such habitats and restoration of the areas for use by waterfowl and other aquatic birds.

In other areas, such as land that is seriously damaged or nearly destroyed by strip mining, careful but expensive habitat restoration can bring such areas to some degree of wildlife productivity, even if not reflective of the original wildlife types that lived there. Nevertheless, varied populations of birds and other wildlife often use restored habitat on former strip-mined land. Fortunately, within recent years, various laws require strip-mined land to be restored as part of mining operations. The companies working the mines carry out much of the restoration work and pay for the costs involved. But even in these circumstances, local birdwatchers may be able to recommend actions that might help locally endangered species.

Other examples of wildlife habitat that is either restored or actually created are marshes and ponds for use by waterfowl, plantings of pine and other trees which eventually form woodland, and prairie grassland restorations. Many such efforts are the joint results of actions of various state and/or federal governmental agencies such as wildlife agencies, soil conservation service officials, forestry departments, and the like. Even in large-scale and expensive professional efforts, however, local bird-watchers sometimes can provide valuable information on former bird populations of an area, particularly nongame species, or census newly created areas to document changes in the birdlife over a period of years.

COOPERATIVE EFFORTS

When professional or governmental agencies are not involved in wildlife habitat restoration projects, local organizations including service clubs, scouts, 4-H organizations, sportsmen's groups, and similar groups of people sometimes can cooperate and combine their efforts to save or restore habitat. Local birdwatchers should play an important part in such programs, and place particular emphasis on the living requirements of nongame species of birds, as well as game species. And, when professional wildlife conservationists are involved in projects, amateur birders can complete routine tasks and free the professionals to devote more time to the more difficult and demanding aspects of a project.

PUBLIC RELATIONS

One of the most important areas in which birdwatchers can play important roles in local endangered species projects is that involving public relations. It is important to keep the general public fully informed of the objectives of such projects, as well as successes or failures experienced as the projects are underway. In addition, public relations efforts can help to increase support (moral and financial) for such efforts. Skilled use of radio, television, magazines, and newspapers are the most obvious ways to gain public exposure. But others also are available. For example, birdwatchers who also are nature photographers can prepare slide programs about such projects for presentation to service clubs (and perhaps obtain financial support from such groups), schools, churches, senior citizen meetings and housing units, and other groups. In addition, sometimes it is possible to arrange to take interested groups of persons on special guided tours of selected project sites to gain further public appreciation and understanding for the effort.

COOPERATION WITH EDUCATORS

In addition to purely public relations activities, birdwatchers involved with locally endangered species projects should make serious efforts to work with local educators to develop teaching units on locally endangered species, and endangered species generally, for use in science programs in area schools. Objectives of the programs can be explained, lists of reference materials—books, charts, films, and slides—can be prepared and supplied to local educators. It also may be necessary to present special in-service teacher workshops where all aspects of such projects can be outlined more fully.

COOPERATION WITH LOCAL GOVERNMENTAL OFFICIALS

Generally local governmental officials are not involved directly in wildlife conservation matters, but there is no reason why they should not be. Birdwatchers can and should take opportunities to discuss locally endangered species projects with such officials and gain their support (or detailed reasons for lack of it), particularly if government property is involved in a project. In some instances, park department crews or other persons such as city foresters can provide helpful and valuable assistance.

BUSINESS AND INDUSTRY

All too frequently wildlife conservationists look upon business and industry as the main threats to birdlife and other wildlife because of development of wildlife habitat for building or other commercial activities. To a considerable degree, there is good reason for this skeptical attitude. Nevertheless, not all business and industry executives and firms are blind to the needs of local wildlife, and sometimes communication with executives of firms will produce funds and technical support for saving vital areas or locally endangered species. Utility companies often are more or less interested in developing wildlife use and conservation areas on some of their properties—often more as a matter of good public relations than any real concern for wildlife conservation—but despite motives such help can be important if locally endangered species are concerned. Thus communication and discussion with business and industry should never be neglected when launching efforts to save locally endangered birdlife.

SERVICE GROUPS

Still another important potential source of people and skills in working on locally endangered species projects are organizations of sportsmen, scouts, 4-H groups, senior citizens, and the like. Senior citizens, in particular, may be most helpful but rarely are because they are not asked! Yet a wide variety of technical and professional persons fall among the ranks of senior citizens, and some of these people might welcome opportunities to again use their years of experience to assist projects dealing with wildlife and endangered species. Thus birdwatchers should contact local senior citizens centers (perhaps located through governmental agencies on the aging or health care organizations) and discuss needs with representatives of these groups. Not all aspects of endangered species projects involve outdoor work. Office and clerical skills also are needed, as are legal and other professional skills, so there can be a wide variety of opportunities open to interested persons.

RETIRED PERSONS

In addition to more or less formal approaches to senior citizen groups, it sometimes is possible to privately contact individual retired wildlife professionals with special wildlife knowledge. Perhaps they can assist endangered species projects on a limited basis with some parts of selected projects. The training and years of experience of such retired persons could perhaps make the difference between success and failure of some projects. Thus birdwatchers should not neglect these people.

PUBLIC HEARINGS

When major federal construction projects are proposed, such as highways and dams, federal law requires the agencies involved in the projects to publish an environmental impact statement (EIS), the purpose of which is to determine accurately and honestly the impact of the proposed project upon the environment. All too often, however, the Army Corps of Engineers and other agencies produce careless, incomplete, and sometimes misleading environmental impact statements, in the hope that the requirements of the law can be satisfied. Attention to wildlife resources, especially nongame wildlife and plants and locally endangered species, rarely receives adequate (or any) study. Only slightly better is consideration given to game species. The result is that far too many projects are built without knowing the full environmental impact of the project upon birds, mammals, and other wildlife and plants of the area. Rare species, including locally endangered birds and other wildlife, can be destroyed entirely and outstanding bird-watching locations frequently are ruined, when they could have been saved and protected if appropriate actions were used.

In large measure, birdwatchers have themselves to blame for the loss of such areas and resources. There is opportunity for all concerned persons to voice their comments verbally or in writing during announced public-comment periods on a project's EIS. Not infrequently, for those projects that are very large and controversial, public hearings also are held at which citizens (not only those living in the vicinity of the project) have opportunities to comment on the projects and the validity and quality of the EIS. That is the time to call specific attention to faults in the EIS and the time to add new information to the public record—especially if it refutes positions or information contained in the EIS or stated by the agency and proponents responsible for the proposed project.

Particular attention should be given to the failure of the agency preparing the EIS to include information already published in existing references such as books and journals, as well as unpublished (but available) information preserved in natural history museums, state museums, universities and colleges, and other public institutions. Frequently such information is neglected despite its direct influence on the project.

Bird clubs, Audubon societies, and wildlife-related organizations, plus individual birdwatchers and wildlife conservationists, can attend hearings and comment upon proposed projects. They can *insist* that agencies and politicians make decisions on a solid environmental basis, rather than on a basis of pork-barrel politics. Wildlife is important in its own right as part of the living fabric of the earth and deserves to live. Let us speak up on its behalf!

LEGISLATIVE RECOMMENDATIONS

In addition to active participation at public hearings, birdwatchers and organizations concerned with birds and other wildlife resources also can influence policies at various levels of government, including local government, by meeting with elected officials at which time new types of legislation can be discussed and recommended for introduction to legislative bodies. When such presentations are based upon facts, few politicians would be foolish enough to ignore the actions being requested. That is particularly true if the persons at the meetings represent well-known conservation organizations which are willing to back their requests with action.

Additional meetings can be held with elected officials to discuss pending legislation and projects and their possible benefit or damage to wildlife and its habitat. The important point is that governmental officials become aware that citizens in their community want solid environmental policies and laws and birds and other wildlife preserved and protected.

In most instances, such meetings with governmental officials can be conducted in an orderly manner. Occasionally, however, intensive political action is necessary to force such persons to act. Indeed, on more than one occasion, politicians have lost office due to the political activism of bird and wildlife enthusiasts who refused to accept the positions taken by politicians on environmental matters.

ADMINISTRATIVE RECOMMENDATIONS

Not all government progress in environmental protection is based upon legislation action. Many worthwhile advances providing for protection of birds and other wildlife habitat, and the environment generally, is achieved as a result of administrative recommendations leading to agency directives or regulations. How receptive a particular agency is toward recommendations coming from private citizens or organizations depends entirely upon the attitudes of the officials of the agencies with which one deals. Sometimes great advances can be made in wildlife conservation with a minimum of effort, simply by meeting with officials and outlining a course of action. All too frequently, however, such recommendations from outside sources are received with hostility and lack of cooperation—and no action to benefit wildlife. Under those circumstances, one is faced with a difficult and often impossible situation. One either can forget about the suggestion, regardless of how worthy it is, or prepare to do battle with the officials.

Among the techniques that sometimes are successful in gaining agency cooperation are public exposure of lack of cooperation via use of radio and television, articles in newspapers and magazines, and presentation of such situations in public lectures. Additional tools include letters, telephone calls, and meetings with elected officials in which one's position is presented clearly and with force. Sometimes enlisting the aid of schoolchildren in letter-writing campaigns to officials and legislators is extremely effective. Most officials cringe at the thought of refusing to cooperate with sincere, concerned children! Black and white photographs, 35mm color slides, and motion pictures also are very effective tools that can add to the effectiveness of one's meetings with officials and other persons in authority. Above all, however, constant public pressure upon agencies is vital when one experiences lack of agency cooperation.

Regardless of what actions are used, it is important that birdwatchers not forget that their object is to save endangered birds

and other wildlife. That is their basic objective when working on
locally endangered species projects.

ADDITIONAL READING

Heintzelman, D. S.
    1971   Rare or Endangered Fish and Wildlife of New Jersey. *Science
           Notes* No. 4. New Jersey State Museum, Trenton, N. J.
    1976   Endangered or Threatened Birds and Mammals of Lehigh
           County, Pennsylvania. *Conservation Report* No. 1. Lehigh
           Valley Audubon Society, Emmaus, Pa.
LaBastille, A.
    1980   *Assignment: Wildlife*. E. P. Dutton, New York, N. Y.

Chapter 11

Promoting Bird Appreciation

Since 1934, when Roger Tory Peterson published the first edition of his classic *A Field Guide to the Birds,* millions of Americans and Canadians have developed some degree of interest in wild birds. Yet millions of other Americans and Canadians do not know about the joy of observing wild birds and have little or no appreciation of these colorful and fascinating creatures with which we share the globe. Here, then, is an excellent opportunity for bird-watchers to engage in public relations projects and activities designed to stimulate increased public interest and appreciation in our native birdlife and its conservation.

There are, of course, many ways in which people can be stimulated to develop an interest in birds and an appreciation of them. Here are some of the more obvious techniques that birdwatchers might wish to use.

PHOTOGRAPHS

Displays of color or black and white photographs of wild birds can be effective and delightful ways in which to stimulate public appreciation of birds. An obvious use of 35mm slides of birds, for example, is the presentation of illustrated lectures to schools, organizations, and other gatherings of people. A thirty-to-sixty-minute program (rarely longer) can bring birds into the lives of people who never previously looked at these animals or gave them serious consideration. With details about their survival and conservation discussed during the program, many people begin to develop an appreciation of birds.

Photographs also add interest and impact to articles published in newspapers or magazines and thus develop more public appreciation of birds. Who can resist enjoying a clear photograph of a hawk in flight? Or a close-up of a bird feeding its young or carrying food to the nestlings? Most people never see such events in the lives of birds. Photography gives them brief views of the lives of wildlife with which we share the globe.

Sometimes local television stations use 35mm color slides of birds in association with special programs. Birdwatchers who have such photographs available should make that fact known to local stations so these resources can be called upon from time to time. In one instance, for example, I used bird slides on local television to show the viewing public what wildlife would be lost if a federal dam was constructed near my home. I selected dramatic close-ups of birds, mammals, and wildflowers so that thousands of people became aware of the needs of wildlife and the fact that a part of our local wildlife heritage was about to disappear if a needless and very costly federal project was built. Bird photography can, indeed, become a potent conservation tool.

Wall posters also can be made from good bird photographs. This technique, too, can be employed to attract public attention to special species of birds of particular interest. In 1981, for example, the United States Fish and Wildlife Service produced a full color poster of a Peregrine Falcon. A variety of Peregrine life history and conservation information was printed in nontechnical language on the back of the poster, and several drawings of Peregrine Falcons in flight, falcon habitat, and related scenes supplemented the textual information. The poster was provided to the public without charge and is suitable for use in school classrooms, at scout meetings, summer camps, sportsmen's clubs, and elsewhere where one wishes to illustrate and discuss this endangered species.

In 1982, as part of National Wildlife Week, the National Wildlife Federation also produced two attractive, color photographic wall posters illustrating birds of prey. One shows an adult Bald Eagle landing with a "We Care About Eagles" message printed on the background. The back of this poster also contains basic history and ecological information about Bald Eagles, as well as simple drawings. The second poster, also using sixteen color photographs, stresses the caring about eagles theme and illustrates four major groups of eagles and their food chain requirements. The back of this poster also presents basic information, in English and Spanish, about the biology and ecology of the eagles depicted on the poster.

Any species of birds, of course, could be the subject of similar posters. Conservation programs designed to help bluebirds, for example, might make a very attractive and useful poster. So, too, would posters dealing with waterfowl, shorebirds, owls, wood warblers, or other common garden birds. While the use of color photography and printing is desirable, it is not always necessary and excellent black and white photographs might be used for some posters. Local birdwatchers who also have photographic and/or commercial art training and experience could combine efforts to create very worthwhile productions. A local bird club could then agree to pay for the printing costs of such posters. In addition to advancing public appreciation of the birds illustrated, the local club also would gain some recognition for its efforts.

Postcards also can serve to show people the beauty of wild birds. I discussed the hobby of collecting bird postcards in an earlier chapter, but here the value of such cards as promotional tools and conservation-education aids can be stressed. In one course on hawk watching, for example, I provided each student with a postcard showing a California Condor in color. I then discussed the plight of this critically endangered species and the various efforts currently in use to try to save the species from extinction. Each student appreciated the condor's fight for survival more by being able to see a color picture of the species.

Birdwatchers and local bird clubs also have excellent opportunities to use postcards to advance their bird conservation efforts. Some do already. Hawk Mountain Sanctuary, for example, sells postcards of birds of prey to visitors. So, too, do many nature centers and other wildlife conservation centers. But relatively few local bird clubs have issued their own postcards for sale to members and others on which pictures of bird species of particular local concern (perhaps locally endangered species) are shown. Here, then is an excellent opportunity to use good photographs taken by local members, art talent of other members, perhaps writing skills of still others, all combined into one local production. If color is too expensive, black and white postcards can be made by local printers.

DRAWINGS AND PAINTINGS

Drawings and paintings of birds, especially those done by local wildlife artists, also can be used in many ways to advance public appreciation of birds. One obvious way, for example, is to hold an annual wildlife art show in a local auditorium or other building. At such events a series of booths would permit local and other wildlife artists, decoy carvers, photographers, and others to display their work. In those parts of the country where such exhibits have been held, the public reaction always is overwhelmingly favorable. Thousands of people visit the shows—even during the first year, if adequate media exposure is provided prior to the opening of the show. And in those instances where the shows are well established, as in Easton and Salisbury, Maryland, and in Philadelphia, Pennsylvania, tens of thousands of people attend during the weekends the shows are open to the public. It is difficult to determine how much impact such art has upon the advancement of bird appreciation, but certainly it is considerable in view of the many people that sometimes travel hundreds of miles to visit such shows and buy items offered for sale there.

Another type of worthwhile wildlife art show is an outdoor show with birds and other wildlife as the theme of the drawings, paintings, carvings, photographs, and other items. Relatively few of these have been held, but where they have, the results were very successful. Local bird clubs could thus profit by organizing such shows in their areas, working in close cooperation with local bird artists, photographers, authors, and others involved with producing materials dealing with wild birds.

Drawings and paintings of wild birds also can be very useful in other ways when promoting bird appreciation. For example, the work of bird artists might be made into special limited-edition prints for fund-raising efforts by a local bird club. Art work also might be used to illustrate educational materials, articles, or any of the other uses for which illustration is desirable. If a nationally recognized bird artist lives locally, perhaps his or her work might be used (with proper permission in writing) in such local conservation-education efforts. Occasionally such artists will agree to prepare a special drawing or painting especially for the launching of a local project. That can be of even more importance and benefit, since collectors all across the country might wish to buy copies, which adds to the success of the local effort. Donations of art objects for public auction also can produce badly needed funds for bird conservation projects.

EXHIBITS

Public exhibits dealing with some aspect of birds also are important promotion and education tools. Exhibits containing photographs, drawings, paintings, specimens, or other aspects of birdlife can be set up in schools, museums, nature centers, county agricultural fairs, and other public meeting places. Sometimes the object is simply to show and name local species. At other times a more special object is aimed at, perhaps food habits of hawks and owls, migration routes used by common local birds, recreational bird-watching equipment, or any number of other aspects of the biology, ecology, conservation, or study of birds. In general, however, it is wise to keep the design of an exhibit very simple and the text explaining it very brief. Nevertheless, birdwatchers can help to develop such exhibits by adding their knowledge to the theme and factual information contained in the display.

SPECIAL EVENTS

Birdwatchers also have excellent opportunities to coordinate and lead special events dealing with birds for the benefit of the general public. A particularly appropriate time to engage in this sort of project is during those periods of the year when special days, weeks, or months are proclaimed by various government officials or agencies.

The annual Hawk Watching Week in Pennsylvania, for example, gives birdwatchers across the state a superb tool to use as a wedge to offer public hawk-watching field trips to local lookouts, seminars about birds of prey and their importance in wildlife communities, discussions and lectures about raptor conservation and the threats faced by raptors in Pennsylvania, as well as across North America and in foreign countries where some of the birds spend their winters.

National Bald Eagle Day can be used to teach people about eagles generally and our national bird in particular. But great care also must be taken to stress the danger that people can inflict upon eagles if they approach the birds closer than about one-quarter mile.

National Wildlife Week can serve as the basis for presenting a host of exhibits, lectures, seminars, field trips, and workshops dealing with a wide variety of topics related to birds. What better opportunity, for instance, to present information about locally endangered species and the projects used to try to help them survive?

Unfortunately, in the past, most birdwatchers—as well as many wildlife refuges—have failed to grasp the value of such special events and have therefore missed excellent opportunities to use a promotional tool that could have advanced public appreciation of birds. Worse still, some birdwatchers have refused to use such special events because of petty politics among associates. One can only hope that such situations are exceptions rather than the rule among conservationists!

Of course, one does not have to have a special event in order to engage in special programs designed to stimulate increased public appreciation of birds. What one does need, however, is enough imagination to design, arrange for, and present such events.

Birdwatchers might well discuss these opportunities with officials of their own bird clubs and arrange to establish a committee (if none already exists) whose task and responsibility it is to arrange for such events.

Special events involving some aspect of bird appreciation also provide birdwatchers with excellent opportunities to prepare special educational teaching kits for distribution to local schoolteachers, scout leaders, and others working with students of all ages. The information contained in such kits would relate to the topic of a poster that would be included in the kit, but among the basics could be a course outline for various age levels, a suggested reading list, and recommendation for using additional visual aids or other teaching aids that might be available or obtained without difficulty.

STAMPS

Earlier in this book, I discussed the hobby of collecting postage and other stamps featuring pictures of birds. It is worthwhile here, however, to discuss the use of postage and other stamps as a means of promoting public appreciation of birds.

The most obvious way in which stamps can be used for this purpose is to simply mail letters using bird stamps. But much more can be done. For example, when new postal issues are released containing portraits of birds, local bird clubs and birdwatchers can arrange public educational events and press conferences designed to build on the theme of the stamp but placing the emphasis on local situations. Birdwatchers rarely have done this and therefore missed excellent opportunities to advance public appreciation of birds.

Similar use of non-postage stamps, such as the splendid wildlife stamps issued by the National Wildlife Federation, also provides birdwatchers with educational and promotional opportunities. At the same time, why not ask the postal service to issue commemorative stamps honoring important bird conservation events? While many such requests are not honored—probably because of lack of political and public support—some may occasionally be accepted and result in the issue of a new postage stamp. When that happens, a carefully coordinated and extensive effort should be made by all birdwatchers across America to use the event to promote bird appreciation and conservation. Just such a use of the spectacular issue of birds of the states stamps in 1982 resulted not only in newspaper and magazine coverage, but also national television coverage. Millions of Americans thus were exposed to birds through postage stamps, including countless persons who never previously gave any consideration to birds and their beauty or needs. Clearly, stamps of one sort or another can help to develop appreciation of birds if birdwatchers and other conservationists have adequate imagination to use them as promotional tools.

RADIO AND TELEVISION

Use of the electronic media is one of the most effective ways in which large numbers of people can be reached and the message of the importance of bird appreciation and conservation presented. Television, by far, is the most effective, since both the spoken word and pictures can be presented. Yet relatively few birdwatchers and bird clubs have taken advantage of this promotional tool. In my own area, for example, I have occasionally used local television to discuss waterfowl, birds of prey, and to fight the construction of a federal dam in the area. But rarely (if ever) have local bird clubs used television for similar purposes. The point is clear. Birdwatchers and bird clubs can make much better and more extensive use of television in advancing bird appreciation and conservation.

On a national basis, birds have done better in getting air time. Many specials dealing wholely, or in part, with birds and their conservation have been broadcast over the years. Recently, for example, the Public Broadcasting System presented "A Field Guide to Roger Tory Peterson" which provided viewers with an excellent (although slightly outdated) summary of Roger Peterson's work and impact upon bird appreciation and conservation in the United States and around the world.

Radio, too, is relatively neglected by most local bird clubs and birdwatchers. Nevertheless, there are some notable exceptions. In Reading, Pennsylvania, for example, Jack Holcomb reached thousands of people in his area using radio on station WEEU, and for some years he had a daily radio program devoted entirely to birds and bird watching. It was one of the most popular programs that station offered—until the station managers decided to cancel the program and replace it with a general call-in talk show! Nevertheless, some bird-related questions still are received and, thus, an even wider audience of people who never previously considered birds or their importance are unavoidably listening to (and learning from) Holcomb's discussions about birds and their needs.

Occasionally I also used local radio and news broadcasts to discuss bird conservation—sometimes the impact of pesticide spraying on birds and other wildlife, sometimes the impact of dam construction on all wildlife, and several times the importance of the effort to secure National Hawk Watching Week when a national effort was underway to secure that special event. I would urge local birdwatchers across America, therefore, to contact local radio stations and try to arrange for programs dealing with local aspects of bird appreciation and conservation whenever possible. Radio is a medium that is neglected far too frequently by the bird-watching community.

CLOTHING

Another way in which birdwatchers can promote public appreciation of birds is to place the message on clothing. T-shirts generally are the most commonly used items for this purpose. One can silk screen the name of a local bird club, hawk-watching effort, loon conservation project, or any other message one wishes onto the shirt. A hawk-watching enthusiast might prepare T-shirts reading "Enjoy Hawk Watching" or "Protect Birds of Prey" to promote these objectives. A bluebird conservationist might put "Save Bluebirds" on a shirt. A waterfowl conservationist might stress "Save Wetlands and Waterfowl" on T-shirts, and members of the North American Loon Fund (Humiston Building, Main Street, Meredith, New Hampshire 03253) certainly will want at least one of their splendid T-shirts showing two loons.

Other items of clothing on which pictures of birds can be placed include men's ties, belt buckles, and jackets. The opportunity is there, if birdwatchers want to use the technique.

Birdwatcher and radio announcer Jack Holcomb has spent more than 14 years providing bird and other wildlife information to listeners of WEEU/850 Radio in Reading, Pennsylvania. Use of radio is an important means of promoting bird appreciation. Photo courtesy of WEEU/850 Radio.

In a similar manner, bird conservation or appreciation messages can be printed on tote bags, table place mats, doormats, and similar items and then sold at fairs, booths, lectures, and other fund-raising activities. While this sort of promotional activity will not in itself save birds or their habitats, the messages reach many people in this way. To some extent, therefore, it helps to advance the education of the general public about birds, their beauty, needs, and conservation.

DONATING BOOKS TO PUBLIC LIBRARIES

Books and birdwatchers go together well and an enormous amount of bird-watching and ornithological literature has developed for North America in particular, and the Americas generally, during the past two centuries. Thus the types of bird books that birders read and enjoy are as varied as birds themselves. Some are field guides, others life history studies or species monographs. Family monographs, distributional studies and checklists, state and other regional bird books, volumes on anatomy, physiology, evolution, ecology, and a host of other topics also are of interest. The very fact that so many bird books are available makes it necessary for most people, however, to select the books they buy carefully.

Public libraries, on the other hand, should be able to collect many more bird books than the average person can. But many public libraries in the United States, particularly in small towns, have little money to spend on bird books and thus have little material on birds on their collections. In some instances the libraries have only two or three bird books, and these may not even include one of the modern field guides to bird identification! Birdwatchers can help to improve this sort of situation by donating bird books to public libraries as one way of promoting public appreciation of birds. So, too, can bird clubs involved in local community affairs.

To some extent reviews of books in the many bird-watching magazines published in North America *might* be helpful when considering which books to donate to a library, but in recent years many thoughtless and incompetent reviews have appeared in such magazines—reviews that frequently reflect the bias of the reviewer or his or her politics rather than the merits of the book being considered. Whenever possible, therefore, examine bird books yourself to determine if they fill your needs or those of the library. There are many levels of interest among birdwatchers, and a book that meets the needs of one person may not be suited to those of another birdwatcher for one reason or another. Libraries need bird books aiding all levels of interest in birds.

What to include in a basic collection of bird books is a matter of considerable difference of opinion, however, despite recommendations published by the editors of *American Birds* in their October 1976 issue. Nevertheless, I agree with the editors that at least one book in each of the following categories be included in a library of bird books.

1. One or more copies of at least one of the general field guides to identification of North American birds.

2. A copy of the most recent or authoritative state or regional bird book published for a particular geographic area.

3. A volume providing a general survey of the families of birds of the world.

4. An ornithology textbook such as one used for undergraduate classes in colleges or universities.

5. Topical books dealing with any particular specific subject for library users, such as birds of prey or hawk migrations.

6. Several literary books dealing with birds and bird watching.

Birdwatchers seeking the titles of such books can refer to *Books in Print,* available in almost all public libraries, or to *A Manual for Bird Watching in the Americas* (chapter 3) which lists most of the essential reference books useful to birdwatchers in the Americas. Reading the article "Choosing a basic ornithological library," published in the October 1976 issue of *American Birds,* also might be helpful.

ADDITIONAL READING

Arbib, R. S.
   1976a   Choosing a Basic Ornithological Library. *American Birds,*
            30 (5): 1009–1015.
   1976b   The Master List of Bird Books for North American Readers.
            American Birds, 30 (5): 1016–1018.
Drennan, S. R.

1976   An Annotated Selection of Regional Bird Books. *American Birds*, 30 (5): 1018–1023.

Heintzelman, D. S.
1979   *A Manual for Bird Watching in the Americas*. Universe Books, New York, N. Y.

Life History Outline

This outline for conducting a typical life history study of a species of bird is based largely upon the table of contents of *Studies in the Life History of the Song Sparrow* by Margaret Morse Nice.

Selected Species as a Study Subject
    Suitability as a Study Object
    Summary of the Life History
    Techniques used in the Investigation
        Trapping Methods
        Banding Methods
            Fish and Wildlife Service Leg Bands
            Color Bands
        Keeping Records and Notes
            Banding Records
            Card Catalog
            Daily Records
            Field Note Books
            Maps
            Nest Records

Incubation
    Role of Female
        Length of Incubation
        Rhythm of Incubation
    Role of Male
Care of Nestlings
    Young in the Nest
    Intervals Between Broods
Nesting Success and Failure
    Number of Young Fledged per Pair in One Season
    Size of Sets and Size of Broods
    Degree of Successfulness of Broods
    Reasons for Loss of Eggs and Young
Survival of Adults
    Adult Males
    Adult Females
    Losses and Replacements in the Population
    Proportion of First-Year Birds in the Population
Survival of the Young
    Return of Fledged Young
        Number of Nestlings that Returned
        Distances from Birth Place where Young Settle
        Return of Young to Birth Place
    Survival of Fledged Young
        Percentage of Fledged Young Surviving One Year
Age Attained by Species
    Average Age of the Species
    Potential Age of the Species
    Age Composition of the Species Population
    Mortality Factors
Development of Young of the Species
    Stages of Development in the Nest
    Fledging
Activities of the Young
    Behavior toward Parents
    Independent Feeding Reactions
    Defecation
    Care of Plumage
    Locomotion

Male and His Mate
    Prenuptial Stage
    Preliminary State
Nest
    Selecting the Site
    Building the Nest
    Meaning of the Nest
Eggs
    Egg Laying
    Incubation
        Role of Female
        Role of Male
        Length of Incubation
    Recognition of Eggs
Care of the Young
    Brooding
    Feeding
    Nest Sanitation
    Recognition of the Young
    Nest Helpers
Defense of Young
    Luring the Young
    Reaction Toward Enemies
    Breakup of Family
Enemy Recognition
    Behavior when Alarmed
    Reaction to Predators

Appendix Two

State Wildlife Agencies

Alabama Division of Game and Fish, 64 N. Union St., Montgomery, Alabama 36130

Alaska Department of Fish and Game, Subport Building, Juneau, Alaska 99801

Arizona Game and Fish Department, 2222 W. Greenway Road, Phoenix, Arizona 85023

Arkansas Game and Fish Commission, 2 Natural Resources Drive, Little Rock, Arkansas 72205

California Department of Fish and Game, 1416 Ninth St., Sacramento, California 95814

Colorado Division of Wildlife, 6060 Broadway, Denver, Colorado 80216

Connecticut Wildlife Unit, State Office Building, 165 Capitol Avenue, Hartford, Connecticut 06115

Delaware Division of Fish and Wildlife, Elward Tatnall Building, P. O. Box 1401, Dover, Delaware 19901

Florida Game and Fresh Water Fish Commission, 620 S. Meridan St., Tallahassee, Florida 32304

Georgia Game and Fish Division, 270 Washington St., SW, Atlanta, Georgia 30334

Hawaii Division of Fish and Game, 1151 Punchbowl St., Honolulu, Hawaii 96813

Idaho Fish and Game Department, 600 S. Walnut, Box 25, Boise, Idaho 83707

Illinois Wildlife Resources Division, 605 Stratton Office Building, Springfield, Illinois 62706

Indiana Division of Fish and Wildlife, 608 State Office Building, Indianapolis, Indiana 46204

Iowa Fish and Game Commission, Wallace State Office Building, Des Moines, Iowa 50319

Kansas Fish and Game Commission, Box 54A, RR2, Pratt, Kansas 67124

Kentucky Department of Fish and Wildlife Resources, 1 Game Farm Road, Frankfort, Kentucky 40601

Louisiana Department of Wildlife and Fisheries, 400 Royal St., New Orleans, Louisiana 70130

Maine Department of Inland Fisheries and Wildlife, 284 State St., Augusta, Maine 04333

Maryland Wildlife Administration, Tawes State Office Building, Annapolis, Maryland 21401

Massachusetts Department of Fisheries, Wildlife and Recreational Vehicles, 100 Cambridge St., Boston, Massachusetts 02202

Michigan Wildlife Division, Box 30028, Lansing, Michigan 48909

Minnesota Wildlife Section, 300 Centennial Building, 658 Cedar St., St. Paul, Minnesota 55155

Mississippi Department of Wildlife Conservation, Southport Mall, P. O. Box 451, Jackson, Mississippi 39205

Missouri Wildlife Division, P. O. Box 180, Jefferson City, Missouri 65102

Montana Department of Fish, Wildlife and Parks, 1420 East Sixth, Helena, Montana 59601

Nebraska Game and Parks Commission, 2200 N. 33rd St., P. O. Box 30370, Lincoln, Nebraska 68503

Nevada Department of Wildlife, Box 10678, Reno, Nevada 89520

New Hampshire Fish and Game Department, 34 Bridge St., Concord, New Hampshire 03301

New Jersey Division of Fish, Game and Wildlife, P. O. Box 1809, Trenton, New Jersey 08625

New Mexico Game and Fish Department, Villagra Building, Santa Fe, New Mexico 87503

New York Division of Fish and Wildlife, 50 Wolf Road, Albany, New York 12233

North Carolina Wildlife Resources Commission, Archdale Building, 512 N. Salisbury St., Raleigh, North Carolina 27611

North Dakota State Game and Fish Department, 2121 Lovett Ave., Bismarck, North Dakota 58505

Ohio Division of Wildlife, Fountain Square, Columbus, Ohio 43224

Oklahoma Department of Wildlife Conservation, 1801 N. Lincoln, P. O. Box 53465, Oklahoma City, Oklahoma 73152

Oregon Department of Fish and Wildlife, P. O. Box 3503, Portland, Oregon 97208

Pennsylvania Game Commission, P. O. Box 1567, Harrisburg, Pennsylvania 17120

Rhode Island Division of Fish and Wildlife, 83 Park St., Providence, Rhode Island 02903

South Carolina Wildlife and Marine Resources Department, Building D, Dutch Plaza, Box 167, Columbia, South Carolina 29202

South Dakota Game, Fish and Parks Department, Sigurd Anderson Building, Pierre, South Dakota 57501

Tennessee Wildlife Resources Agency, P. O. Box 40747, Ellington Agricultural Center, Nashville, Tennessee 37204

Texas Parks and Wildlife Department, 4200 Smith School Road, Austin, Texas 78744

Utah Division of Wildlife Resources, 1596 W. N. Temple, Salt Lake City, Utah 84116

Vermont Fish and Game Department, Montpelier, Vermont 05602

Virginia Commission of Game and Inland Fisheries, 4010 W. Broad St., Box 11104, Richmond, Virginia 23230

Washington Department of Game, 600 N. Capitol Way, Olympia, Washington 98504

West Virginia Department of Wildlife Resources, 1800 Washington St., East, Charleston, West Virginia 25305

Wisconsin Bureau of Wildlife Management, Box 7921, Madison, Wisconsin 53707

Wyoming Game and Fish Department, Cheyenne, Wyoming 82002

About the Author

Donald S. Heintzelman has been an Associate Curator of Natural Science at the William Penn Memorial Museum and was for some years Curator of Ornithology at the New Jersey State Museum. Now a wildlife consultant, lecturer, and writer, he has traveled widely in North America, the West Indies, South America, the Falkland and Galapagos Islands, East Africa, and Antarctica studying and photographing wildlife. For many years he was an Audubon Wildlife Film lecturer for the National Audubon Society, and also was ornithologist on board the M. S. *Lindblad Explorer* on voyages to Amazonia, Antarctica, and Galapagos. He has written many books of which *A World Guide to Whales, Dolphins, and Porpoises, The Illustrated Bird Watcher's Dictionary, A Manual for Bird Watching in the Americas, A Guide to Hawk Watching in North America, Hawks and Owls of North America, North American Ducks, Geese & Swans,* and *Autumn Hawk Flights* are the most recent. Mr. Heintzelman also has published numerous notes and articles on ornithology, wildlife and conservation in leading national and international wildlife magazines. Among birds his special interests are birds of prey, waterfowl, and seabirds; among mammals the splendid whales, dolphins, and porpoises. He lives in Allentown, Pennsylvania, not far from the famous Pennsylvania hawk ridges and other important centers of bird watching. From there he travels throughout the world on wildlife projects.

Index